Part I: Getting Started with Excel VBA and Macros 5

  1. Introduction to Excel VBA and Macros 5

    What is VBA? 5

    Understanding Macros 6

    Why Use VBA and Macros in Excel? 6

    Overview of the Excel 2024 and 365 Interface 7

    Setting Up Your VBA Environment 8

  2. Recording and Running Macros 10

    Introduction to Macro Recorder 10

    Recording Your First Macro 10

    Running Macros 11

    Managing Macros: The Macro Dialog Box 12

    Assigning Macros to Buttons, Menus, and Keyboard Shortcuts 13

  3. Introduction to the VBA Editor 15

    Navigating the VBA Editor 15

    Code Windows and Project Explorer 16

    Understanding Modules, Classes, and UserForms 17

    Writing Your First VBA Code 19

  4. Basic Programming Concepts In VBA 21

    Variables, Constants, and Data Types 21

    Operators and Expressions 22

    Control Structures: If...Then, Select Case 24

    Loops: For, For Each, Do While, Do Until 26

    Procedures and Functions 28

Part II: Automating Excel Tasks with VBA and Macros 31

  5. Working with Excel Objects 31

    The Excel Object Model 31

    Understanding Workbooks and Worksheets 32

    Range and Cell Objects 33

    Using Collections: Worksheets, Charts, and Shapes 35

Working with Named Ranges and Tables 36

6. Manipulating Data with VBA 38

Automating Data Entry and Validation 38

Sorting and Filtering Data Programmatically 40

Importing and Exporting Data 42

Working with Text Files and CSVs 44

Automating PivotTables and Charts 47

7. Creating and Managing UserForms 50

Introduction to UserForms 50

Designing UserForms: Controls and Layout 50

Programming UserForm Events 52

Data Validation and Input Handling 53

Creating Dynamic UserForms 55

8. Debugging and Error Handling in VBA 58

Types of Errors in VBA 58

Debugging Tools in the VBA Editor 60

Using Breakpoints and Watch Windows 61

Error Handling Techniques: On Error Resume Next, On Error GoTo 62

Writing Robust Code with Defensive Programming 65

Part III: Advanced VBA Techniques 69

9. Advanced Programming Techniques 69

Working with Arrays and Collections 69

Using Dictionaries in VBA 71

Creating and Using Custom Classes 73

Interacting with Other Office Applications: Word, Outlook, and PowerPoint 75

Accessing External Data Sources: Databases and Web Services 77

10. Optimizing VBA Code for Performance 80

Understanding VBA Performance Bottlenecks 80

Writing Efficient Code: Best Practices 82

Reducing Workbook and Worksheet Calculation Time 84

Working with Large Datasets 85

Memory Management in VBA 87

11. Creating Custom Functions and Add-Ins 90

Writing Custom Worksheet Functions 90

Creating Add-Ins in Excel 92

Distributing and Installing Add-Ins 93

Managing Versions and Updates for Add-Ins 94

Protecting Your Code: Password Protection and Digital Signatures 96

Part IV: Solving Real-World Problems with VBA and Macros 99

12. Automating Financial Models 99

Building Dynamic Financial Models 99

Automating Financial Analysis 102

Creating Custom Financial Reports 104

Case Study: Automated Budgeting Tool 106

13. Data Analysis and Visualization 110

Automating Data Cleaning and Preparation 110

Advanced Data Analysis Techniques 112

Automating the Creation of Dashboards 114

Case Study: Automated Sales Reporting System 116

14. Managing Projects with Excel VBA 120

Automating Project Plans and Schedules 120

Tracking Project Progress with VBA 123

Resource Allocation and Optimization 126

Case Study: Automated Gantt Chart Creation 129

15. Automating Repetitive Tasks in Excel 133

Automating Routine Reporting Tasks 133

Bulk Data Processing with VBA 136

Creating Reusable Macro Libraries 138

Case Study: Automating HR Reports and Payroll Processing 140

Part V: Appendices 145

Appendix A: Common VBA Functions and Their Uses 145

Appendix B: VBA Reference Guide 147

Appendix C: Troubleshooting and FAQs 149

Appendix D: Useful Resources and Further Reading 151

Appendix E: Sample Projects and Solutions 152

Part I: Getting Started with Excel VBA and Macros

1. Introduction to Excel VBA and Macros

Welcome to the world of Excel VBA and Macros, where the power of automation transforms how you interact with data and perform tasks in Excel. Whether you're a beginner looking to streamline daily operations or an experienced user aiming to unlock the full potential of Excel, this chapter will lay the foundation for your journey.

What is VBA?

VBA (Visual Basic for Applications) is a programming language developed by Microsoft, embedded within most Microsoft Office applications, including Excel. VBA allows users to automate repetitive tasks, enhance Excel's functionality, and even create custom applications tailored to specific needs.

Unlike general-purpose programming languages, VBA is designed to be relatively easy to learn and use, particularly for those already familiar with Excel. It's a procedural programming language that interacts directly with Excel's objects—like workbooks, sheets, and ranges—allowing you to control nearly every aspect of the Excel environment.

Key Features of VBA:

- **Automation:** VBA automates repetitive tasks, such as data entry, formatting, and complex calculations.

- **Customization:** You can tailor Excel to your specific needs, creating custom functions, forms, and interfaces.

- **Integration:** VBA integrates Excel with other Microsoft Office applications like Word, Outlook, and Access, and even with external data sources.

Understanding Macros

A **macro** is a sequence of instructions that automate tasks in Excel. When you perform an action like formatting a cell or copying data, you're essentially running a series of steps. A macro captures these steps and allows you to run them automatically with a single command.

How Macros Work:

- **Recording Macros:** Excel provides a built-in macro recorder that captures your actions as you perform them. These actions are then converted into VBA code.

- **Running Macros:** Once recorded, you can execute the macro at any time, replicating the same series of steps without manual intervention.

- **Editing Macros:** You can edit the VBA code behind the macro to fine-tune its behavior, add conditions, or introduce loops and more complex logic.

Macros are a powerful tool for increasing productivity by reducing the time spent on repetitive tasks. For example, if you regularly generate reports that require specific formatting and data manipulation, a macro can handle this for you in seconds.

Why Use VBA and Macros in Excel?

Excel is a versatile tool that offers robust capabilities out of the box, but there are times when its standard functions aren't enough. That's where VBA and macros come in.

Benefits of Using VBA and Macros:

- **Efficiency:** Automate repetitive tasks, freeing up time for more critical activities.

- **Consistency:** Ensure that tasks are performed the same way every time, reducing the risk of human error.

- **Customization:** Tailor Excel to meet your unique requirements, from simple macros to complex, user-friendly applications.

- **Enhanced Functionality:** Go beyond Excel's built-in features, creating new functions, automating complex processes, and integrating with other applications.

Real-World Applications:

- Automating monthly financial reports.

- Creating custom dashboards that update automatically.

- Generating invoices, tracking inventory, and managing projects with minimal effort.

- Integrating Excel with databases, such as Access or SQL Server, for more complex data analysis.

Overview of the Excel 2024 and 365 Interface

Before diving into VBA and macros, it's essential to familiarize yourself with the Excel 2024 and 365 interface, which provides the environment where you'll write, run, and manage your VBA code.

Key Interface Elements:

- **Ribbon:** The Ribbon is your primary toolbar, housing various commands organized into tabs. The "Developer" tab is where you'll find tools related to macros and VBA.

- **Workbook and Worksheets:** Your VBA code will interact with workbooks and worksheets, so it's important to understand how they're structured. Each workbook can contain multiple sheets, each of which is a grid of cells where data is stored.

- **VBA Editor:** Accessed via the Developer tab, the VBA Editor is where you'll write and edit your VBA code. It's a separate environment from Excel but closely integrated, allowing you to interact with your Excel workbooks.

Excel 2024 and 365 Enhancements:

- **Enhanced Developer Tab:** The Developer tab in Excel 2024 and 365 offers improved access to macro tools, making it easier to record, run, and manage macros.

- **Improved Integration with Office 365:** Excel 365 offers seamless integration with other Office 365 applications, enhancing the potential for VBA automation across multiple platforms.

Setting Up Your VBA Environment

Before you start writing VBA code or recording macros, you need to set up your Excel environment to make the most of these tools.

Steps to Set Up Your VBA Environment:

1. **Enable the Developer Tab:**

   o By default, the Developer tab is hidden in Excel. To enable it, go to File > Options > Customize Ribbon and check the "Developer" option.

2. **Access the VBA Editor:**

   o You can access the VBA Editor by clicking on the "Visual Basic" button in the Developer tab. Alternatively, you can press Alt + F11 to open it directly.

3. **Customize the VBA Editor:**

   o The VBA Editor is highly customizable. You can adjust the layout of windows like the Project Explorer, Properties Window, and Code Window to suit your workflow.

   o Consider setting up custom shortcuts and adjusting the editor's font size for better readability.

4. **Set Macro Security Settings:**

   o Excel has security settings that may block macros from running. Go to Developer > Macro Security to adjust these settings. While it's important to keep your system secure, enabling macros from trusted sources is essential for using VBA.

5. **Test Your Setup:**

   o Create a simple test macro to ensure everything is set up correctly. For example, record a macro that formats a cell, and then view the generated VBA code in the editor.

By the end of this chapter, you should have a solid understanding of what VBA and macros are, why they are invaluable tools in Excel, and how to set up your environment to start automating tasks. In the next chapters, we will dive deeper into recording macros, navigating the VBA Editor, and writing your first VBA code.

2. Recording and Running Macros

In this chapter, you will learn how to record and run macros in Excel, a fundamental skill for automating tasks without writing a single line of code. We'll start by introducing the Macro Recorder, then guide you through recording your first macro, running it, managing macros using the Macro Dialog Box, and finally assigning macros to buttons, menus, and keyboard shortcuts for easy access.

Introduction to Macro Recorder

The **Macro Recorder** is a powerful tool that captures your actions in Excel and translates them into VBA code. It's an excellent way to start automating tasks, especially if you're not yet comfortable writing code. The Macro Recorder is perfect for automating repetitive tasks, such as formatting cells, entering data, or applying filters.

Key Features of the Macro Recorder:

- **Ease of Use:** No coding knowledge required—simply perform your tasks, and the recorder captures your steps.

- **Efficiency:** Automates tasks that would otherwise be repetitive and time-consuming.

- **Learning Tool:** Provides insight into how actions in Excel translate to VBA code, making it a great tool for learning VBA.

However, it's essential to note that while the Macro Recorder is powerful, it records everything you do, including any mistakes or unnecessary steps. This can sometimes lead to inefficient or overly complex code, which is why learning to edit and refine the recorded macros is crucial.

Recording Your First Macro

Let's start by recording your first macro. In this example, we'll record a simple task: formatting a range of cells.

Steps to Record a Macro:

1. **Enable the Developer Tab:**

- o If you haven't done so already, enable the Developer tab by going to **File** > **Options** > **Customize Ribbon**, and check the "Developer" option.

2. **Start the Macro Recorder:**

- o Click on the **Developer** tab, then select **Record Macro**. A dialog box will appear, asking for details about your macro.

3. **Name Your Macro:**

- o In the "Macro name" field, give your macro a descriptive name (e.g., **FormatCells**). Remember, macro names must start with a letter and cannot contain spaces.

- o Optionally, you can assign a shortcut key by entering it in the "Shortcut key" field. Be careful to choose a key combination that doesn't conflict with existing Excel shortcuts.

4. **Store Your Macro:**

- o Choose where to store your macro. You can store it in the current workbook, in your **Personal Macro Workbook** (to make it available in all workbooks), or in a new workbook.

5. **Add a Description (Optional):**

- o Enter a brief description of what the macro does. This is especially helpful for future reference or when sharing the macro with others.

6. **Perform the Actions:**

- o Once you click **OK**, the recorder starts capturing every action you take in Excel. For this example, select a range of cells, apply a specific format (e.g., bold font, yellow fill color), and maybe adjust the column width.

7. **Stop Recording:**

- o After completing your actions, go back to the **Developer** tab and click **Stop Recording**. Your macro is now saved and ready to use.

Running Macros

Now that you've recorded your first macro, running it is just as easy. You can execute macros directly from the Developer tab, assign them to buttons, or use keyboard shortcuts.

Steps to Run a Macro:

1. **Run via the Developer Tab:**

   o   Go to **Developer > Macros**. This will open the Macro Dialog Box, where you can see a list of all available macros.

   o   Select the macro you just recorded (**FormatCells**), and click **Run**.

2. **Run with a Keyboard Shortcut:**

   o   If you assigned a shortcut key while recording the macro, you can simply use that key combination to run the macro.

   o   For example, if you set **Ctrl + Shift + F** as the shortcut, pressing those keys will instantly run your macro.

3. **Run from the Macro Dialog Box:**

   o   Access the Macro Dialog Box by pressing **Alt + F8**. This method is useful if you have multiple macros and want to select one to run.

Running a macro is an efficient way to apply consistent formatting or perform repetitive tasks across different ranges or sheets without having to repeat the steps manually.

Managing Macros: The Macro Dialog Box

The **Macro Dialog Box** is the central hub for managing all your recorded macros. It provides options to run, edit, delete, or assign macros to buttons and other interface elements.

Using the Macro Dialog Box:

1. **Opening the Macro Dialog Box:**

   o   You can access the Macro Dialog Box by clicking **Developer > Macros** or by pressing **Alt + F8**.

2. **Navigating the Dialog Box:**

   o The dialog box lists all available macros in the current workbook, personal macro workbook, or other open workbooks.

   o Select a macro from the list to view its options.

3. **Running a Macro:**

   o Simply select the macro and click **Run**.

4. **Editing a Macro:**

   o Click **Edit** to open the VBA Editor, where you can view and modify the macro's code. This is useful for making adjustments or optimizing the code generated by the Macro Recorder.

5. **Deleting a Macro:**

   o If you no longer need a macro, select it and click **Delete**. Be careful with this option, as deleted macros cannot be recovered.

6. **Creating a New Macro:**

   o You can also create a new macro directly from this dialog box by clicking **Create**. This opens the VBA Editor, where you can start writing a new macro from scratch.

Assigning Macros to Buttons, Menus, and Keyboard Shortcuts

1. **Add a Button to the Worksheet:**

   o Go to **Developer > Insert**, and select the **Button** option under Form Controls. Click anywhere on the worksheet to place the button.

2. **Assign a Macro to the Button:**

   o After placing the button, the **Assign Macro** dialog box will appear. Select the macro you want to assign (e.g., **FormatCells**) and click **OK**.

3. **Customize the Button:**

   o You can change the text on the button by right-clicking it and selecting **Edit Text**. You can also resize or move the button as needed.

Assigning Macros to the Ribbon or Quick Access Toolbar:

1. **Customize the Ribbon:**

   o Right-click anywhere on the Ribbon and select **Customize the Ribbon**. Here, you can add a new tab or group and then assign your macro to a button within that group.

2. **Add to the Quick Access Toolbar:**

   o Right-click the macro in the Macro Dialog Box, and select **Add to Quick Access Toolbar**. This places the macro on the toolbar at the top of the Excel window for easy access.

Assigning Macros to Keyboard Shortcuts:

1. **Assigning During Macro Recording:**

   o As mentioned earlier, you can assign a shortcut key when first recording the macro.

2. **Assigning to an Existing Macro:**

   o If you didn't assign a shortcut during recording, you can do so by going to **Developer > Macros**, selecting the macro, and clicking **Options**. Here, you can enter or change the shortcut key.

Best Practices for Assigning Macros:

- **Avoid Conflicts:** Be mindful of existing Excel shortcuts when assigning new ones.

- **Organize Custom Buttons:** Group related macros under the same tab or Quick Access Toolbar group for better organization.

- **Document Shortcuts:** Keep a list of your custom shortcuts for quick reference.

3. Introduction to the VBA Editor

The VBA Editor is where the magic happens in Excel automation. It's the environment where you write, edit, and manage the VBA code that powers your macros. Understanding how to navigate the VBA Editor, work with its components, and write your first lines of VBA code is essential for anyone looking to take full advantage of Excel's automation capabilities.

Navigating the VBA Editor

The VBA Editor is a separate application that opens when you start working with VBA in Excel. It might seem intimidating at first, but once you get familiar with its layout and features, you'll find it to be a powerful tool for customizing and automating Excel.

How to Access the VBA Editor:

- You can open the VBA Editor by pressing **Alt + F11** in Excel, or by clicking on **Visual Basic** in the Developer tab.

- The VBA Editor will open in a new window, separate from the main Excel interface.

Key Components of the VBA Editor:

- **Menu Bar:** Similar to other Microsoft applications, the Menu Bar contains various options like File, Edit, View, and Tools. These menus offer commands for managing projects, editing code, and customizing the VBA environment.

- **Toolbar:** Just below the Menu Bar, the Toolbar provides quick access to common commands such as saving, running, and debugging your code.

- **Project Explorer:** Located on the left side of the editor, the Project Explorer is a tree-view window that shows all open workbooks and their associated VBA components, such as modules, classes, and UserForms.

- **Properties Window:** Below the Project Explorer, the Properties Window displays properties for the selected object (like a worksheet or UserForm). You can modify these properties directly from this window.

- **Code Window:** The main area where you'll write and edit your VBA code. Each module, class, or UserForm has its own Code Window.

- **Immediate Window:** A debugging tool where you can test code snippets and evaluate expressions in real-time.

Understanding the layout and functionality of these components is the first step toward mastering the VBA Editor. Now, let's take a closer look at some of these elements.

Code Windows and Project Explorer

The **Project Explorer** and **Code Windows** are two of the most important parts of the VBA Editor. They help you navigate through different parts of your VBA projects and write the code that drives your macros.

Project Explorer:

- The Project Explorer is essentially the "home base" of the VBA Editor. It displays all the objects that make up your Excel project, including workbooks, worksheets, modules, and UserForms.

- Each workbook has its own folder in the Project Explorer. Within this folder, you'll find objects like **ThisWorkbook**, which represents the workbook itself, and **Sheet1**, **Sheet2**, etc., representing individual worksheets.

- You'll also find **Modules**, which are containers for your VBA code. When you record a macro, Excel automatically creates a module to store the associated VBA code.

Navigating the Project Explorer:

- Click the plus (+) sign next to a workbook's name to expand its contents.

- Double-click on any object (e.g., a module or worksheet) to open its Code Window.

- Use the search box at the top of the Project Explorer to quickly find specific objects.

Code Windows:

- The Code Window is where you write and view your VBA code. When you double-click a module, worksheet, or workbook in the Project Explorer, its associated Code Window opens.

- Each object can have its own set of procedures (subroutines or functions) written in its Code Window. For example, you might have a macro that runs when a particular worksheet is activated, and the code for this would be written in that worksheet's Code Window.

Working with Code Windows:

- You can have multiple Code Windows open simultaneously, allowing you to work on different parts of your project at the same time.

- If your code becomes lengthy, you can use the **View > Procedure View** or **Full Module View** options to toggle between viewing a single procedure or the entire module.

- The Code Window also includes a handy drop-down list at the top, allowing you to navigate between different procedures within the same module quickly.

Understanding Modules, Classes, and UserForms

In VBA, your code is organized into **Modules, Classes**, and **UserForms**. Each serves a different purpose and plays a specific role in your VBA projects.

Modules:

- **Standard Modules:** These are the most common type of modules where you'll write most of your macros. When you record a macro, Excel automatically creates a standard module (usually named **Module1, Module2**, etc.) and places the macro code inside.

- **Procedures:** Within a standard module, code is organized into procedures. A procedure is a block of VBA code that performs a specific task. There are two types of procedures:

  o **Sub Procedures (Subroutines):** Perform actions, such as formatting a worksheet or calculating a value. They are written using the **Sub** keyword.

  o **Function Procedures (Functions):** Return a value after performing calculations or operations. They are written using the **Function** keyword.

- **Example of a Sub Procedure:**

```
Sub FormatCells()
    Range("A1:A10").Font.Bold = True
    Range("A1:A10").Interior.Color = RGB(255, 255, 0)
End Sub
```

Classes:

- **Class Modules:** Unlike standard modules, class modules are used to create custom objects and define their properties, methods, and events. Class modules are more advanced and are typically used when you need to create objects that encapsulate data and functionality together.

- **Object-Oriented Programming:** Class modules allow you to use principles of object-oriented programming (OOP) in VBA, such as creating objects with attributes and behaviors that can interact with other objects.

- **Example of a Class Module:**

  o Suppose you're building an inventory system, and you want to define a custom **Product** class with properties like **Name**, **Price**, and **Quantity**. A class module would be used to create this **Product** object.

UserForms:

- **UserForms:** These are custom dialog boxes or forms that you create to interact with users. UserForms can include controls like text boxes, buttons, combo boxes, and more, allowing for complex data entry and user interactions.

- **Designing UserForms:** In the VBA Editor, you can design UserForms using a drag-and-drop interface to place controls onto the form. Each control can then be programmed to perform specific actions using VBA code.

- **Example of a UserForm:**

  o Imagine you want to collect user input for a report, such as a date range and specific criteria. You can create a UserForm that pops up when the macro runs, allowing the user to enter this information.

Using Modules, Classes, and UserForms Together:

- Often, a VBA project will involve multiple modules, classes, and UserForms working together. For example, a standard module might handle the main processing logic, a class module could represent custom data objects, and a UserForm could collect user input.

Writing Your First VBA Code

Now that you're familiar with the VBA Editor and its components, it's time to write your first VBA code. In this section, we'll walk through creating a simple macro from scratch.

Creating a New Module:

1. In the Project Explorer, right-click on the workbook name where you want to add the code.

2. Select **Insert > Module**. A new module will appear under the workbook in the Project Explorer, and a new Code Window will open.

Writing a Simple Macro:

- Let's write a macro that displays a message box when it's run.

Steps:

1. In the Code Window, type the following code:

```
Sub ShowMessage()
    MsgBox "Hello, welcome to VBA!"
End Sub
```

2. This code defines a **Sub** procedure named **ShowMessage**. When the macro runs, it displays a message box with the text "Hello, welcome to VBA!"

Running the Macro:

1. To run the macro, go back to Excel and press **Alt + F8** to open the Macro Dialog Box.

2. Select **ShowMessage** from the list of macros and click **Run**.

3. A message box should appear with your custom message.

Congratulations! You've just written and executed your first VBA macro. While simple, this example introduces the core concepts of VBA: writing procedures, interacting with Excel objects, and running code.

Conclusion

In this chapter, you've been introduced to the VBA Editor, learned how to navigate its components, and explored the role of modules, classes, and UserForms in VBA. You also wrote your first VBA macro, gaining hands-on experience with the code-writing process.

With these foundational skills, you're now ready to delve deeper into the world of Excel automation, creating more complex macros, and developing custom solutions tailored to your needs. In the next chapters, we'll explore more advanced VBA programming techniques, helping you to unlock the full potential of Excel.

4. Basic Programming Concepts in VBA

Understanding the basic programming concepts in VBA is essential to writing efficient and effective code. This chapter will introduce you to the fundamental building blocks of VBA, including variables, constants, data types, operators, expressions, control structures, loops, procedures, and functions. These concepts will serve as the foundation for more advanced programming techniques you'll learn later in the book.

Variables, Constants, and Data Types

Variables are used in VBA to store data that can change during the execution of a program. They act as placeholders for information that your code will manipulate, such as numbers, text, or object references.

Declaring Variables:

- In VBA, you declare a variable using the Dim statement, followed by the variable name and its data type.

- Example:

```
Dim total As Integer
Dim itemName As String
Dim isAvailable As Boolean
```

Naming Conventions:

- Variable names should be descriptive and meaningful, helping to make your code more readable.

- They must begin with a letter, can include letters and numbers, and cannot contain spaces or special characters (except underscores).

Data Types:

- VBA supports various data types, each designed to store specific kinds of data. Choosing the correct data type is important for optimizing memory usage and improving code performance.

    o **Integer:** Stores whole numbers between -32,768 and 32,767.

    o **Long:** Stores larger whole numbers between - 2,147,483,648 and 2,147,483,647.

21

- o **Single:** Stores single-precision floating-point numbers.

- o **Double:** Stores double-precision floating-point numbers.

- o **String:** Stores text.

- o **Boolean:** Stores **True** or **False**.

- o **Date:** Stores dates and times.

- o **Variant:** Can store any type of data; however, it's generally less efficient and should be used sparingly.

Example of Using Variables:

```
Dim quantity As Integer
Dim price As Double
Dim totalCost As Double

quantity = 10
price = 19.99
totalCost = quantity * price
MsgBox "The total cost is " & totalCost
```

Constants:

- **Constants** are similar to variables, but their value remains unchanged throughout the execution of the program.

- You declare a constant using the **Const** keyword.

- Example:

```
Const pi As Double = 3.14159
Const maxStudents As Integer = 30
```

Using constants makes your code easier to maintain, as you can update the constant's value in one place without having to change it throughout the code.

Operators and Expressions

Operators are symbols that specify the type of operation to perform on operands in an expression. VBA includes various operators for arithmetic, comparison, concatenation, and logical operations.

Arithmetic Operators:

- + (Addition)

- - (Subtraction)

- * (Multiplication)

- / (Division)

- ^ (Exponentiation)

- **Mod** (Modulus, returns the remainder of a division)

Example:

```
Dim result As Double
result = (5 + 3) * 2 ^ 2 ' Result is 32
```

Comparison Operators:

- = (Equal to)

- < (Less than)

- > (Greater than)

- <= (Less than or equal to)

- >= (Greater than or equal to)

- <> (Not equal to)

Example:

```
Dim isEqual As Boolean
isEqual = (10 = 5) ' Result is False
```

String Concatenation Operator:

- **&** (Concatenates two strings)

Example:

```
Dim greeting As String
greeting = "Hello, " & "World!" ' Result is "Hello,
World!"
```

Logical Operators:

- **And** (True if both conditions are true)

- **Or** (True if at least one condition is true)

- **Not** (Inverts the truth value)

Example:

```
Dim check As Boolean
check = (5 > 3) And (10 < 20) ' Result is True
```

Expressions:

- **Expressions** are combinations of variables, constants, operators, and functions that return a value.

- Example:

```
Dim area As Double
area = pi * (radius ^ 2) ' Calculates the area of a circle
```

Understanding how to use operators and expressions effectively is crucial for performing calculations, making decisions, and manipulating data in your VBA programs.

Control Structures: If...Then, Select Case

Control structures are used to control the flow of your VBA program based on conditions. The two primary control structures in VBA are **If...Then** and **Select Case**.

If...Then Structure:

- The **If...Then** structure executes a block of code if a specified condition is true.

- You can use **Else** to define an alternative block of code to execute if the condition is false.

- **ElseIf** allows you to check multiple conditions.

Syntax:

```
If condition Then
    ' Code to execute if condition is true
ElseIf anotherCondition Then
```

```
        ' Code to execute if anotherCondition is true
    Else
        ' Code to execute if all conditions are false
    End If
```

Example:

```
    Dim score As Integer
    score = 85


    If score >= 90 Then
        MsgBox "Grade: A"
    ElseIf score >= 80 Then
        MsgBox "Grade: B"
    ElseIf score >= 70 Then
        MsgBox "Grade: C"
    Else
        MsgBox "Grade: F"
    End If
```

Select Case Structure:

- The **Select Case** structure is an alternative to **If...Then** when you have multiple possible values for a single expression.

- It is often easier to read and manage than multiple **If...Then** statements.

Syntax:

```
    Select Case expression
        Case value1
            ' Code to execute if expression equals value1
        Case value2
            ' Code to execute if expression equals value2
        Case Else
            ' Code to execute if expression does not match any
    value
    End Select
```

Example:

```
    Dim dayOfWeek As Integer
```

```
dayOfWeek = Weekday(Date)

Select Case dayOfWeek
    Case 1
        MsgBox "Sunday"
    Case 2
        MsgBox "Monday"
    Case 3
        MsgBox "Tuesday"
    Case 4
        MsgBox "Wednesday"
    Case 5
        MsgBox "Thursday"
    Case 6
        MsgBox "Friday"
    Case 7
        MsgBox "Saturday"
    Case Else
        MsgBox "Invalid day"
End Select
```

Using control structures allows you to make decisions within your code, enabling your VBA programs to handle a variety of scenarios dynamically.

Loops: For, For Each, Do While, Do Until

Loops allow you to repeat a block of code multiple times, which is especially useful for tasks like processing collections of data, iterating through ranges, or performing repeated calculations.

For...Next Loop:

- The **For...Next** loop is used to repeat a block of code a specific number of times.

Syntax:

```
For counter = start To end [Step stepValue]
    ' Code to execute in each iteration
Next counter
```

Example:

```
Dim i As Integer

For i = 1 To 10
    Cells(i, 1).Value = "Row " & i
Next i
```

For Each...Next Loop:

- The For Each...Next loop is used to iterate over all elements in a collection, such as all cells in a range or all worksheets in a workbook.

Syntax:

```
For Each element In collection
    ' Code to execute for each element
Next element
```

Example:

```
Dim ws As Worksheet

For Each ws In ThisWorkbook.Worksheets
    MsgBox ws.Name
Next ws
```

Do While Loop:

- The **Do While** loop continues to execute a block of code as long as a specified condition is true.

Syntax:

```
Do While condition
    ' Code to execute while condition is true
Loop
```

Example:

```
Dim counter As Integer
counter = 1

Do While counter <= 5
    MsgBox "Counter is " & counter
```

```
counter = counter + 1
Loop
```

Do Until Loop:

- The **Do Until** loop continues to execute a block of code until a specified condition becomes true.

Syntax:

```
Do Until condition
    ' Code to execute until condition becomes true
Loop
```

Example:

```
Dim counter As Integer
counter = 1

Do Until counter > 5
    MsgBox "Counter is " & counter
    counter = counter + 1
Loop
```

Loops are invaluable for automating repetitive tasks, making your code more efficient and reducing the need for manual input

Procedures and Functions

In VBA, code is organized into **Procedures** and **Functions**, which are blocks of code that perform specific tasks. Understanding how to create and use these blocks is crucial for writing organized, reusable code.

Sub Procedures (Subroutines):

- A **Sub procedure** is a block of code that performs actions but does not return a value.

- Sub procedures are used for tasks like formatting cells, copying data, or interacting with the user.

Syntax:

```
Sub ProcedureName()
    ' Code to execute
```

```
        End Sub
```

Example:

```
    Sub GreetUser()
        MsgBox "Welcome to VBA!"
    End Sub
```

Functions:

- A **Function** is similar to a Sub procedure, but it returns a value after performing its task.

- Functions are used for calculations or operations that produce a result, such as mathematical computations or string manipulations.

Syntax:

```
    Function FunctionName([arguments]) As DataType
        ' Code to execute
        FunctionName = result
    End Function
```

Example:

```
    Function AddNumbers(a As Double, b As Double) As Double
        AddNumbers = a + b
    End Function
```

Calling Procedures and Functions:

- You can call a Sub procedure from another Sub or Function by simply using its name:

```
    Call GreetUser
```

Or:

```
    GreetUser
```

- To use a function, you typically assign its return value to a variable or use it in an expression:

```
    Dim result As Double
    result = AddNumbers(5, 3) ' Result is 8
    MsgBox "The sum is " & result
```

Passing Arguments:

- Both procedures and functions can accept arguments, which are inputs passed to them when they are called. This makes your code more flexible and reusable.

- Arguments can be passed **by value** (default), meaning that the procedure receives a copy of the variable, or **by reference**, meaning that the procedure can modify the original variable.

Example of Passing Arguments:

```
Sub DisplayMessage(message As String)
    MsgBox message
End Sub


Call DisplayMessage("Hello, VBA!")
```

Organizing Code with Procedures and Functions:

- By organizing your code into procedures and functions, you create modular code that is easier to maintain, debug, and reuse. This approach promotes good programming practices and makes your VBA projects more manageable.

Part II: Automating Excel Tasks with VBA and Macros

5. Working with Excel Objects

Excel VBA provides you with the tools to automate tasks, and a key aspect of this is understanding how to work with Excel's objects. Objects in Excel are the fundamental building blocks of any VBA code, allowing you to interact with workbooks, worksheets, ranges, cells, and more. In this chapter, we'll explore the Excel Object Model, how to work with workbooks and worksheets, manipulate ranges and cells, use collections to manage groups of objects, and effectively handle named ranges and tables.

The Excel Object Model

The **Excel Object Model** is a hierarchical structure that represents all the elements in Excel, such as the application itself, workbooks, worksheets, ranges, and cells. Understanding this model is crucial because it helps you navigate and manipulate these objects through VBA.

Hierarchy of the Excel Object Model:

1. **Application:** The top-level object, representing the entire Excel application.

2. **Workbooks:** A collection of all open workbooks.

3. **Workbook:** A single workbook within the Workbooks collection.

4. **Worksheets:** A collection of all worksheets within a workbook.

5. **Worksheet:** A single worksheet within the Worksheets collection.

6. **Range:** A cell or a group of cells within a worksheet.

Navigating the Object Model:

- To interact with these objects, you typically start from the top of the hierarchy (Application) and drill down to the specific object you want to manipulate.

31

- However, in most cases, you don't need to reference the **Application** object directly, as it is implied. For example, **ThisWorkbook** refers to the workbook where the VBA code is running, and **ActiveSheet** refers to the currently active worksheet.

Example:

```
Dim ws As Worksheet
Set ws = ThisWorkbook.Sheets("Sheet1")
ws.Range("A1").Value = "Hello, World!"
```

In this example, you start by referencing **ThisWorkbook**, then drill down to the specific worksheet ("Sheet1"), and finally to the range ("A1") to set its value.

Understanding Workbooks and Worksheets

Workbooks and **Worksheets** are among the most commonly used objects in Excel VBA. A workbook is essentially the Excel file, while worksheets are the individual sheets within that file where data is stored and manipulated.

Working with Workbooks:

- To work with a specific workbook, you can refer to it using the **Workbooks** collection.

- Example of opening a workbook:

```
Dim wb As Workbook
Set wb = Workbooks.Open("C:\Path\To\Your\Workbook.xlsx")
```

- Example of creating a new workbook:

```
Dim wb As Workbook
Set wb = Workbooks.Add
```

Referencing Workbooks:

- You can refer to workbooks by their name:

```
Set wb = Workbooks("WorkbookName.xlsx")
```

- Or you can use **ThisWorkbook** to refer to the workbook containing the VBA code, or **ActiveWorkbook** to refer to the workbook currently in focus.

Saving and Closing Workbooks:

- Example of saving a workbook:

```
wb.Save
wb.SaveAs "C:\Path\To\NewWorkbook.xlsx"
```

- Example of closing a workbook:

```
wb.Close SaveChanges:=True
```

Working with Worksheets:

- Worksheets are accessed through the **Worksheets** collection of a workbook.

- Example of referencing a worksheet:

```
Dim ws As Worksheet
Set ws = ThisWorkbook.Sheets("Sheet1")
```

- Example of adding a new worksheet:

```
Dim ws As Worksheet
Set ws =
ThisWorkbook.Sheets.Add(After:=ThisWorkbook.Sheets(ThisWor
kbook.Sheets.Count))
```

- Example of renaming a worksheet:

```
ws.Name = "NewSheetName"
```

Activating and Selecting Worksheets:

- Example of activating a worksheet:

```
ws.Activate
```

- Example of selecting a worksheet (note: **Select** is rarely needed):

```
ws.Select
```

Understanding how to manage workbooks and worksheets is fundamental to automating tasks in Excel. Whether you're opening files, creating new sheets, or organizing your data, these objects form the core of your VBA projects.

Range and Cell Objects

The **Range** object is perhaps the most important object in Excel VBA, representing a cell or a group of cells. Almost everything you do in Excel involves interacting with ranges, whether it's reading data, writing to cells, formatting, or performing calculations.

Referencing Ranges:

- The most straightforward way to reference a range is by specifying the cell address:

```
Dim rng As Range
Set rng = ws.Range("A1")
```

- To reference a range of cells:

```
Set rng = ws.Range("A1:B10")
```

- You can also reference a single cell using **Cells**:

```
Set rng = ws.Cells(1, 1) ' Refers to A1
```

Working with Range Properties:

- **Value:** To get or set the value of a range:

```
rng.Value = "Hello"
MsgBox rng.Value
```

- **Address:** To get the address of a range:

```
MsgBox rng.Address
```

- **Rows and Columns:** To refer to rows or columns within a range:

```
Dim rowRange As Range
Set rowRange = rng.Rows(1) ' First row in the range
```

Using Offset and Resize:

- **Offset:** Moves the reference to a different cell relative to the original range:

```
Set rng = rng.Offset(1, 0) ' Moves down one row
```

- **Resize:** Changes the size of the range:

```
Set rng = rng.Resize(2, 2) ' Resizes to a 2x2 range
```

Performing Actions on Ranges:

- **Formatting:** You can change the appearance of cells:

```
rng.Font.Bold = True
rng.Interior.Color = RGB(255, 255, 0) ' Yellow background
```

- Copying and Pasting:

```
rng.Copy Destination:=ws.Range("C1")
```

- Clearing Content or Formatting:

```
rng.ClearContents
rng.ClearFormats
```

Mastering the Range object is key to automating Excel effectively, as it enables you to manipulate data at a granular level, perform calculations, and control cell formatting with precision.

Using Collections: Worksheets, Charts, and Shapes

Collections in VBA are groups of related objects that you can manipulate together. For example, the **Worksheets** collection includes all the worksheets in a workbook, while the **Charts** and **Shapes** collections include all the charts and shapes, respectively.

Working with the Worksheets Collection:

- To loop through all worksheets in a workbook:

```
Dim ws As Worksheet
For Each ws In ThisWorkbook.Worksheets
    MsgBox ws.Name
Next ws
```

Working with the Charts Collection:

- Adding a chart to a worksheet:

```
Dim chartObj As ChartObject
Set chartObj = ws.ChartObjects.Add(Left:=100, Width:=375, Top:=50, Height:=225)
chartObj.Chart.SetSourceData Source:=ws.Range("A1:B10")
```

Working with the Shapes Collection:

- Adding a shape to a worksheet:

```
Dim shp As Shape
Set shp = ws.Shapes.AddShape(msoShapeRectangle, 100, 50, 200, 100)
shp.Fill.ForeColor.RGB = RGB(255, 0, 0) ' Red background
```

Using the For Each Loop with Collections:

- Looping through all shapes in a worksheet:

```
Dim shp As Shape
```

```
For Each shp In ws.Shapes
    MsgBox shp.Name
Next shp
```

Collections simplify the process of managing groups of similar objects, making it easier to perform bulk operations, such as formatting all worksheets or moving all shapes.

Working with Named Ranges and Tables

Named Ranges and **Tables** are powerful features in Excel that enhance the clarity and usability of your spreadsheets. They allow you to reference ranges or tables by name, making your VBA code more readable and easier to manage.

Named Ranges:

- Creating a named range:

```
ThisWorkbook.Names.Add Name:="SalesData",
RefersTo:=ws.Range("A1:A10")
```

- Referencing a named range in VBA:

```
Dim rng As Range
Set rng = ws.Range("SalesData")
```

- Using named ranges makes your code more readable and reduces the likelihood of errors caused by hard-coding cell references.

Tables:

- Excel tables (also known as ListObjects) are structured ranges that include special features like sorting, filtering, and automatic formatting.

- Creating a table from a range:

```
Dim tbl As ListObject
Set tbl = ws.ListObjects.Add(xlSrcRange,
ws.Range("A1:B10"), , xlYes)
tbl.Name = "SalesTable"
```

- Referencing a table in VBA:

```
Set tbl = ws.ListObjects("SalesTable")
```

- Accessing table data:

```
Dim tblRange As Range
Set tblRange = tbl.DataBodyRange
MsgBox "Number of rows: " & tblRange.Rows.Count
```

Working with Table Columns:

- You can reference specific columns in a table by their name:

```
Dim col As ListColumn
Set col = tbl.ListColumns("Product")
col.DataBodyRange.Font.Bold = True
```

Named ranges and tables enhance the structure of your Excel data and make your VBA code more intuitive and easier to maintain. They are particularly useful in larger projects where data needs to be organized and referenced consistently.

6. Manipulating Data with VBA

Data manipulation is at the heart of most Excel tasks, and VBA provides powerful tools to automate these processes. Whether you need to automate data entry, validate data, sort and filter information, import and export files, or generate PivotTables and charts, VBA can handle it all efficiently. This chapter will guide you through the essential techniques for manipulating data with VBA, giving you the ability to automate complex workflows and ensure data accuracy.

Automating Data Entry and Validation

One of the most common tasks in Excel is data entry. While manual entry can be time-consuming and prone to errors, VBA allows you to automate this process, ensuring consistency and saving time. Additionally, data validation ensures that only correct and relevant data is entered, reducing the likelihood of mistakes.

Automating Data Entry:

- **Simple Data Entry:** You can use VBA to automate the entry of data into specific cells or ranges. This is particularly useful when you need to populate cells based on certain criteria or input from the user.

  Example:

```
Sub EnterData()
    Dim ws As Worksheet
    Set ws = ThisWorkbook.Sheets("DataEntry")

    ws.Range("A1").Value = "Product ID"
    ws.Range("B1").Value = "Product Name"
    ws.Range("C1").Value = "Quantity"

    ws.Range("A2").Value = 101
    ws.Range("B2").Value = "Laptop"
    ws.Range("C2").Value = 5
End Sub
```

- **User Input:** VBA can prompt users for input using the **InputBox** function, then enter that data into the worksheet automatically.

Example:

```vba
Sub UserDataEntry()
    Dim ws As Worksheet
    Set ws = ThisWorkbook.Sheets("DataEntry")

    Dim productID As Integer
    Dim productName As String
    Dim quantity As Integer

    productID = InputBox("Enter Product ID:")
    productName = InputBox("Enter Product Name:")
    quantity = InputBox("Enter Quantity:")

    ws.Range("A2").Value = productID
    ws.Range("B2").Value = productName
    ws.Range("C2").Value = quantity
End Sub
```

Automating Data Validation:

- **Adding Validation Rules:** You can automate data validation by applying validation rules to cells or ranges using VBA. This ensures that the data entered meets specific criteria, such as being within a certain range or matching a particular format.

Example:

```vba
Sub AddDataValidation()
    Dim ws As Worksheet
    Set ws = ThisWorkbook.Sheets("DataEntry")

    With ws.Range("C2:C100").Validation
        .Delete
        .Add Type:=xlValidateWholeNumber,
AlertStyle:=xlValidAlertStop, _
            Operator:=xlBetween, Formula1:="1",
Formula2:="100"
        .InputTitle = "Enter Quantity"
        .ErrorTitle = "Invalid Entry"
```

```
        .InputMessage = "Please enter a quantity between 1
and 100."
        .ErrorMessage = "The value must be a whole number
between 1 and 100."
    End With
End Sub
```

- **Checking Data Validity:** You can also write VBA code to check if the data entered into a worksheet meets the desired criteria, providing feedback to the user if it doesn't.

Example:

```
Sub ValidateData()
    Dim ws As Worksheet
    Set ws = ThisWorkbook.Sheets("DataEntry")
    Dim quantity As Integer

    quantity = ws.Range("C2").Value

    If quantity < 1 Or quantity > 100 Then
        MsgBox "Quantity must be between 1 and 100",
vbExclamation
        ws.Range("C2").Select
    Else
        MsgBox "Data is valid", vbInformation
    End If
End Sub
```

Automating data entry and validation not only speeds up the process but also ensures that your data is accurate and consistent, reducing the need for manual corrections.

Sorting and Filtering Data Programmatically

Sorting and filtering data are essential tasks when managing large datasets. With VBA, you can automate these processes to quickly organize and retrieve the information you need.

Sorting Data:

- **Basic Sorting:** You can use the **Sort** method to sort data in ascending or descending order based on one or more columns.

    Example:

    ```
    Sub SortData()
        Dim ws As Worksheet
        Set ws = ThisWorkbook.Sheets("DataEntry")

        ws.Range("A1:C100").Sort Key1:=ws.Range("A2"),
    Order1:=xlAscending, Header:=xlYes
    End Sub
    ```

- **Multi-Level Sorting:** VBA allows you to sort data on multiple levels, such as first by Product ID, then by Quantity.

    Example:

    ```
    Sub MultiLevelSort()
        Dim ws As Worksheet
        Set ws = ThisWorkbook.Sheets("DataEntry")

        ws.Range("A1:C100").Sort _
            Key1:=ws.Range("A2"), Order1:=xlAscending, _
            Key2:=ws.Range("C2"), Order2:=xlDescending, _
            Header:=xlYes
    End Sub
    ```

Filtering Data:

- **Applying Filters:** You can automate the process of filtering data to display only the rows that meet specific criteria.

    Example:

    ```
    Sub FilterData()
        Dim ws As Worksheet
        Set ws = ThisWorkbook.Sheets("DataEntry")

        ws.Range("A1:C100").AutoFilter Field:=3,
    Criteria1:=">=10"
    End Sub
    ```

- **Clearing Filters:** Once you're done working with filtered data, you can clear the filters programmatically.

Example:

```
Sub ClearFilters()
    Dim ws As Worksheet
    Set ws = ThisWorkbook.Sheets("DataEntry")

    If ws.AutoFilterMode Then
        ws.AutoFilterMode = False
    End If
End Sub
```

By automating sorting and filtering, you can quickly organize and analyze your data, enabling you to focus on decision-making rather than manual data manipulation.

Importing and Exporting Data

Importing data from external sources and exporting data from Excel are common tasks that can be automated with VBA, streamlining the process of data integration and reporting.

Importing Data:

- **Importing from Another Workbook:** You can use VBA to pull data from another Excel workbook into the current one.

Example:

```
Sub ImportData()
    Dim ws As Worksheet
    Set ws = ThisWorkbook.Sheets("DataEntry")

    Dim sourceWb As Workbook
    Set sourceWb =
Workbooks.Open("C:\Path\To\SourceWorkbook.xlsx")

    sourceWb.Sheets("Sheet1").Range("A1:C100").Copy
Destination:=ws.Range("A1")
    sourceWb.Close SaveChanges:=False
```

```
        End Sub
```

- **Importing from a Text File:** VBA can also be used to import data from a text file, such as a CSV file, into Excel.

Example:

```
Sub ImportCSV()
    Dim ws As Worksheet
    Set ws = ThisWorkbook.Sheets("DataEntry")

    Open "C:\Path\To\Data.csv" For Input As #1

    Dim rowNum As Integer
    rowNum = 1

    Dim lineData As String
    Do While Not EOF(1)
        Line Input #1, lineData
        ws.Cells(rowNum, 1).Value = lineData
        rowNum = rowNum + 1
    Loop

    Close #1
End Sub
```

Exporting Data:

- **Exporting to Another Workbook:** You can export data from the current workbook to a new or existing workbook.

Example:

```
Sub ExportData()
    Dim ws As Worksheet
    Set ws = ThisWorkbook.Sheets("DataEntry")

    Dim exportWb As Workbook
    Set exportWb = Workbooks.Add
```

```
ws.Range("A1:C100").Copy
Destination:=exportWb.Sheets(1).Range("A1")
    exportWb.SaveAs "C:\Path\To\ExportedData.xlsx"
    exportWb.Close SaveChanges:=True
End Sub
```

- **Exporting to a Text File:** You can also export data to a text file, such as a CSV.

Example:

```
Sub ExportCSV()
    Dim ws As Worksheet
    Set ws = ThisWorkbook.Sheets("DataEntry")

    Open "C:\Path\To\ExportedData.csv" For Output As #1

    Dim rowNum As Integer
    For rowNum = 1 To 100
        Print #1, ws.Cells(rowNum, 1).Value & "," &
ws.Cells(rowNum, 2).Value & "," & ws.Cells(rowNum,
3).Value
    Next rowNum

    Close #1
End Sub
```

Automating the import and export of data saves time and reduces the risk of errors that can occur with manual processes, ensuring that your data is accurately integrated and shared across systems.

Working with Text Files and CSVs

Text files and CSVs are commonly used for storing and exchanging data, and VBA offers robust tools for reading from and writing to these file formats.

Reading from Text Files:

- **Line-by-Line Reading:** You can read a text file line by line and process each line as needed.

Example:

```
Sub ReadTextFile()
    Dim filePath As String
    filePath = "C:\Path\To\YourFile.txt"

    Open filePath For Input As #1
    Dim lineData As String

    Do While Not EOF(1)
        Line Input #1, lineData
        MsgBox lineData
    Loop

    Close #1
End Sub
```

- **Reading CSV Files:** Similar to text files, CSV files can be read into Excel, with each line being split into cells based on the delimiter.

Example:

```
Sub ReadCSV()
    Dim filePath As String
    filePath = "C:\Path\To\YourFile.csv"

    Open filePath For Input As #1
    Dim lineData As String
    Dim rowNum As Integer
    rowNum = 1

    Dim fields As Variant
    Do While Not EOF(1)
        Line Input #1, lineData
        fields = Split(lineData, ",")
        Cells(rowNum, 1).Resize(1, UBound(fields) +
1).Value = fields
        rowNum = rowNum + 1
    Loop
```

```
        Close #1
End Sub
```

Writing to Text Files:

- **Writing Data to a Text File:** You can easily export data from Excel into a text file using VBA.

  Example:

```
Sub WriteTextFile()
    Dim filePath As String
    filePath = "C:\Path\To\YourFile.txt"

    Open filePath For Output As #1
    Print #1, "This is a sample text file."
    Print #1, "Exported from Excel using VBA."

    Close #1
End Sub
```

- **Writing to CSV Files:** Similarly, you can export Excel data to a CSV file.

  Example:

```
Sub WriteCSV()
    Dim filePath As String
    filePath = "C:\Path\To\YourFile.csv"

    Open filePath For Output As #1
    Dim rowNum As Integer

    For rowNum = 1 To 100
        Print #1, Cells(rowNum, 1).Value & "," &
Cells(rowNum, 2).Value & "," & Cells(rowNum, 3).Value
    Next rowNum

    Close #1
End Sub
```

Working with text files and CSVs through VBA allows you to seamlessly exchange data between Excel and other applications, making your workflows more versatile and integrated.

Automating PivotTables and Charts

PivotTables and charts are powerful tools for summarizing and visualizing data in Excel. Automating their creation and manipulation with VBA can save significant time and ensure consistency in your reports.

Creating and Manipulating PivotTables:

- **Creating a PivotTable:** You can automate the creation of PivotTables, specifying the data source, location, and fields to be used.

  Example:

```
Sub CreatePivotTable()
    Dim ws As Worksheet
    Set ws = ThisWorkbook.Sheets("PivotSheet")

    Dim dataRange As Range
    Set dataRange =
ThisWorkbook.Sheets("DataEntry").Range("A1:C100")

    Dim pivotCache As PivotCache
    Set pivotCache =
ThisWorkbook.PivotCaches.Create(SourceType:=xlDatabase,
SourceData:=dataRange)

    Dim pivotTable As PivotTable
    Set pivotTable =
ws.PivotTables.Add(PivotCache:=pivotCache,
TableDestination:=ws.Range("A3"), TableName:="SalesPivot")

    With pivotTable
        .PivotFields("Product Name").Orientation =
xlRowField
        .PivotFields("Quantity").Orientation = xlDataField
    End With
```

```
End Sub
```

- **Updating PivotTables:** Once a PivotTable is created, you can update it programmatically whenever the underlying data changes.

Example:

```
Sub UpdatePivotTable()
    Dim ws As Worksheet
    Set ws = ThisWorkbook.Sheets("PivotSheet")

    ws.PivotTables("SalesPivot").PivotCache.Refresh
End Sub
```

Creating and Customizing Charts:

- **Creating a Chart:** VBA allows you to create charts dynamically based on your data and customize their appearance.

Example:

```
Sub CreateChart()
    Dim ws As Worksheet
    Set ws = ThisWorkbook.Sheets("ChartSheet")

    Dim chartObj As ChartObject
    Set chartObj = ws.ChartObjects.Add(Left:=100,
Width:=375, Top:=50, Height:=225)

    With chartObj.Chart
        .SetSourceData Source:=ws.Range("A1:B10")
        .ChartType = xlColumnClustered
        .HasTitle = True
        .ChartTitle.Text = "Sales Data"
    End With
End Sub
```

- **Customizing Chart Elements:** You can further customize the chart by modifying its axes, legend, data labels, and more.

Example:

```
Sub CustomizeChart()
```

```
Dim ws As Worksheet
Set ws = ThisWorkbook.Sheets("ChartSheet")

With ws.ChartObjects(1).Chart
    .Axes(xlCategory, xlPrimary).HasTitle = True
    .Axes(xlCategory, xlPrimary).AxisTitle.Text =
"Products"
    .Axes(xlValue, xlPrimary).HasTitle = True
    .Axes(xlValue, xlPrimary).AxisTitle.Text =
"Quantity Sold"
    End With
End Sub
```

Automating the creation and updating of PivotTables and charts with VBA ensures that your data analysis and reports are always accurate and up-to-date, enabling you to focus on interpreting the results rather than on the mechanics of generating them.

By mastering the techniques covered in this chapter, you can significantly enhance your ability to manipulate data in Excel using VBA. From automating data entry and validation to sorting, filtering, importing, exporting, and generating dynamic reports, these skills will empower you to create more efficient, reliable, and insightful Excel applications. In the next chapters, you'll explore even more advanced topics, including creating user interfaces, interacting with other Office applications, and optimizing your VBA code for performance.

7. Creating and Managing UserForms

UserForms in Excel VBA provide a powerful way to create custom dialogs and data entry forms that enhance user interaction with your Excel applications. In this chapter, you will learn how to create and manage UserForms, design effective interfaces using various controls, program UserForm events, handle data validation and input, and create dynamic UserForms that adapt to user inputs.

Introduction to UserForms

A **UserForm** is a custom-built dialog box that you create in Excel VBA to collect information from users, display information, or facilitate interaction with your Excel application. UserForms can be simple, with just a few input fields, or complex, with multiple controls and interactive elements.

Why Use UserForms?

- **Enhanced User Interaction:** UserForms provide a user-friendly way to collect input, guide users through processes, or display complex information.

- **Data Validation:** You can control the data that users enter, ensuring it meets specific criteria before being processed.

- **Custom Interface:** Unlike built-in Excel dialog boxes, UserForms are fully customizable, allowing you to create interfaces that match the specific needs of your application.

Creating a UserForm:

- To create a UserForm, open the VBA Editor (**Alt + F11**), go to **Insert > UserForm**. A new UserForm will appear, and the Toolbox will automatically display a set of controls that you can add to your form.

- The UserForm has its own code module where you can write VBA code to manage events and control the behavior of the form.

Designing UserForms: Controls and Layout

Designing an effective UserForm involves choosing the right controls, organizing them logically, and ensuring a user-friendly layout. The VBA Toolbox provides various controls that you can use to build your UserForm.

Common Controls:

- **Labels:** Used to display text or instructions on the form.

- **TextBox:** Allows users to input text or numbers.

- **ComboBox:** Provides a drop-down list of options for users to select from.

- **ListBox:** Displays a list of items from which users can select one or more.

- **CommandButton:** Used to execute a command, such as submitting the form or canceling an action.

- **CheckBox:** Allows users to make a true/false or yes/no selection.

- **OptionButton (Radio Button):** Used to allow users to select one option from a group.

- **Frame:** Groups related controls together, providing a visual and functional structure.

- **MultiPage:** Allows for multiple pages within the same UserForm, useful for complex forms with different sections.

Designing a UserForm Layout:

- **Aligning Controls:** Use the alignment tools in the VBA Editor to ensure controls are neatly aligned. This improves the appearance and usability of your form.

- **Grouping Controls:** Use frames to group related controls together, which helps users understand the structure of the form and reduces clutter.

- **Setting Tab Order:** The tab order determines the sequence in which controls receive focus when the user presses the **Tab** key. Setting a logical tab order improves the user experience.

Example of a Simple UserForm:

1. Create a new UserForm and add the following controls:

    o   Label1: "Enter your name:"

- o TextBox1: For name input

- o Label2: "Select your department:"

- o ComboBox1: For department selection

- o CommandButton1: "Submit"

- o CommandButton2: "Cancel"

2. Set properties for the controls:

- o Set the **Name** property for each control to something meaningful (e.g., **txtName, cmbDepartment, btnSubmit**).

- o Set the Caption property for labels and buttons to display the appropriate text.

3. Organize the controls in a logical layout on the form.

Programming UserForm Events

UserForms in VBA are event-driven, meaning they respond to user actions like clicking a button, entering text, or selecting an option. By programming these events, you can control the behavior of the form and how it interacts with the user.

Common UserForm Events:

- • **Initialize Event:** Runs when the UserForm is first loaded, typically used to set initial values or populate controls.

  Example:

```
Private Sub UserForm_Initialize()
    cmbDepartment.AddItem "Finance"
    cmbDepartment.AddItem "Marketing"
    cmbDepartment.AddItem "IT"
    cmbDepartment.AddItem "HR"
End Sub
```

- • **Click Event:** Triggered when the user clicks a control, such as a CommandButton.

  Example:

```
Private Sub btnSubmit_Click()
```

```
    MsgBox "Hello " & txtName.Text & " from " &
cmbDepartment.Text
    Me.Hide ' Hides the form after submission
End Sub


Private Sub btnCancel_Click()
    Me.Hide ' Hides the form without taking action
End Sub
```

- **Change Event:** Triggered when the value of a control changes, such as when the user types in a TextBox or selects an item in a ComboBox.

Example:

```
Private Sub txtName_Change()
    If Len(txtName.Text) > 0 Then
        btnSubmit.Enabled = True
    Else
        btnSubmit.Enabled = False
    End If
End Sub
```

Using Event Handlers:

- Event handlers are subroutines that execute in response to events, enabling you to build interactive and responsive forms.

- You can also use event handlers to validate data, update other controls based on user input, or trigger additional actions.

Data Validation and Input Handling

Ensuring that users provide valid data is crucial for the reliability of your Excel applications. Data validation and input handling in UserForms help prevent errors and ensure data integrity.

Validating User Input:

- **Basic Validation:** You can use the **Change** or **Exit** events to validate user input in real-time, providing immediate feedback if the input is invalid.

Example:

```
Private Sub txtName_Exit(ByVal Cancel As
MSForms.ReturnBoolean)
    If Len(txtName.Text) = 0 Then
        MsgBox "Name cannot be empty", vbExclamation
        Cancel = True ' Keeps focus on the TextBox until
valid input is provided
    End If
End Sub
```

- **Conditional Validation:** You can set up conditional validation based on the content of other controls or the current state of the form.

Example:

```
Private Sub btnSubmit_Click()
    If txtName.Text = "" Then
        MsgBox "Please enter your name", vbExclamation
        Exit Sub
    End If

    If cmbDepartment.ListIndex = -1 Then
        MsgBox "Please select a department", vbExclamation
        Exit Sub
    End If

    ' If all validations pass, proceed with the operation
    MsgBox "Form submitted successfully"
    Me.Hide
End Sub
```

Handling Input Errors:

- **Error Messages:** Use message boxes to inform users when they have made an error in their input, guiding them on how to correct it.

- **Input Formatting:** Automatically format user input to match required standards (e.g., converting text to uppercase, adding date formatting).

Example:

```vba
Private Sub txtPhoneNumber_Exit(ByVal Cancel As
MSForms.ReturnBoolean)
    Dim phoneNumber As String
    phoneNumber = txtPhoneNumber.Text

    If Not IsNumeric(phoneNumber) Or Len(phoneNumber) <>
10 Then
        MsgBox "Please enter a valid 10-digit phone
number", vbExclamation
        Cancel = True
    Else
        txtPhoneNumber.Text = Format(phoneNumber, "(###)
###-####")
    End If
End Sub
```

Effective data validation and input handling ensure that your forms are robust and that the data they collect is accurate and reliable.

Creating Dynamic UserForms

Dynamic UserForms are those that change based on user input or other conditions, providing a more interactive and responsive user experience. You can create dynamic forms by adding, removing, or modifying controls at runtime.

Adding Controls at Runtime:

- You can add controls to a UserForm dynamically during runtime based on user actions or external conditions.

    Example:

```vba
Private Sub UserForm_Initialize()
    Dim btnDynamic As MSForms.CommandButton
    Set btnDynamic =
Me.Controls.Add("Forms.CommandButton.1", "btnDynamic",
True)
    btnDynamic.Caption = "Dynamic Button"
    btnDynamic.Top = 100
    btnDynamic.Left = 50
```

```
        btnDynamic.Width = 100
    End Sub
```

Modifying Controls Based on Input:

- You can change the properties of controls dynamically, such as enabling/disabling buttons, changing captions, or updating list options based on other inputs.

    Example:

```
    Private Sub cmbDepartment_Change()
        If cmbDepartment.Text = "IT" Then
            lblExtraInfo.Caption = "Please enter your tech
skills:"
            txtExtraInfo.Visible = True
        Else
            lblExtraInfo.Caption = ""
            txtExtraInfo.Visible = False
        End If
    End Sub
```

Conditional Layout Adjustments:

- You can adjust the layout of the UserForm based on the inputs or selections made by the user. For instance, hiding or showing different sections of the form depending on the user's selections.

    Example:

```
    Private Sub optYesNo_Change()
        If optYes Then
            FrameDetails.Visible = True
            Me.Height = 300 ' Adjust form height to show the
new section
        Else
            FrameDetails.Visible = False
            Me.Height = 200 ' Adjust form height to hide the
section
        End If
    End Sub
```

Dynamic UserForms in Action:

- Dynamic forms are particularly useful for creating wizards, multi-step forms, or forms that need to adapt based on the user's previous choices. This makes your applications more flexible and tailored to the user's needs.

Creating dynamic UserForms allows you to build more responsive and interactive applications that can adapt to different scenarios, improving user engagement and satisfaction.

By the end of this chapter, you should be proficient in creating and managing UserForms in Excel VBA. You've learned how to design user-friendly forms, program event-driven interactions, validate and handle user input, and create dynamic forms that respond to user actions. These skills will enable you to build sophisticated user interfaces for your Excel applications, making them more intuitive and powerful. In the next chapters, you will continue to expand your VBA knowledge by exploring advanced techniques for optimizing your code, integrating with other applications, and more.

8. Debugging and Error Handling in VBA

Programming in VBA, like in any other language, involves writing, testing, and refining code. Inevitably, errors will occur, whether due to logical mistakes, unexpected input, or unforeseen conditions. This chapter will guide you through understanding the types of errors in VBA, utilizing debugging tools, setting breakpoints, using watch windows, and applying effective error-handling techniques. Mastering these skills will help you write more robust, maintainable, and error-resistant code.

Types of Errors in VBA

In VBA, errors can be broadly categorized into three types: **syntax errors, runtime errors,** and **logical errors**. Understanding the nature of these errors is the first step in effectively managing and resolving them.

1. **Syntax Errors:**

    o **What They Are:** Syntax errors occur when the code you've written doesn't conform to the grammatical rules of the VBA language. These errors are typically caught as you type your code, as VBA checks syntax in real-time.

    o **Common Causes:** Missing punctuation, incorrect use of keywords, unmatched parentheses, or incorrect structure.

    o **How to Identify:** VBA's editor will highlight syntax errors immediately, usually by displaying a red line or a pop-up error message.

    o **Example:**

    ```
    Sub CalculateTotal()
        Dim total As Double
        total = 10 + ' Missing second operand
    End Sub
    ```

2. **Runtime Errors:**

    • **What They Are:** Runtime errors occur when the code is syntactically correct but fails during execution. These errors are often due to unforeseen conditions, such as dividing by zero, referencing an object that doesn't exist, or running out of memory.

- **Common Causes:** Invalid operations, file access issues, incorrect data types, or attempting to access a workbook or worksheet that is not available.

- **How to Identify:** VBA will display an error message during execution and typically highlight the offending line of code.

- **Example:**

```
Sub OpenWorkbook()
    Dim wb As Workbook
    Set wb =
Workbooks.Open("C:\Path\NonExistentFile.xlsx") ' Runtime
error if file doesn't exist
End Sub
```

3. **Logical Errors:**

- **What They Are:** Logical errors occur when the code runs without syntax or runtime errors, but produces incorrect results. These are often the most difficult to detect because VBA will not flag them automatically; you'll need to identify them through testing and validation.

- **Common Causes:** Incorrect calculations, misplaced conditions, or wrong loop logic.

- **How to Identify:** Logical errors require careful testing of the code's output and validation against expected results.

- **Example:**

```
Sub CalculateDiscount()
    Dim price As Double
    price = 100
    Dim discount As Double
    discount = price * 0.05 ' Logical error if discount
should be 5% of price
    MsgBox "Discount: " & discount ' Displays incorrect
discount if logic is flawed
End Sub
```

Understanding these errors is crucial for efficiently debugging your code and applying appropriate error-handling strategies.

Debugging Tools in the VBA Editor

The VBA Editor includes several built-in tools designed to help you debug your code. These tools allow you to pause code execution, inspect variables, and step through your code line by line to identify and resolve issues.

Immediate Window:

- The Immediate Window is a versatile tool that allows you to execute VBA commands, evaluate expressions, and print variable values while your code is running.

- **How to Use:** Press Ctrl + G to open the Immediate Window. You can type any VBA expression or command directly and press Enter to execute it.

- **Example:**

  ```
  ? Application.Version ' Displays the version of Excel in
  use
  Debug.Print ActiveSheet.Name ' Prints the active sheet
  name to the Immediate Window
  ```

Locals Window:

- The Locals Window shows the current values of all variables within the current scope. It's useful for monitoring the state of variables as your code executes.

- **How to Use:** Open the Locals Window by going to **View > Locals Window** in the VBA Editor.

- **Example:** As you step through your code, watch how the values of your variables change in the Locals Window.

Call Stack:

- The Call Stack allows you to see the chain of procedures or functions that have been called to reach the current point in your code. This is particularly useful for understanding the sequence of events leading to an error.

- **How to Use:** Open the Call Stack by going to **View > Call Stack** or pressing **Ctrl + L** when an error occurs.

- **Example:** Use the Call Stack to trace back through your procedures to understand how your code reached a certain point.

Debug.Print:

- The **Debug.Print** statement sends output to the Immediate Window, which is helpful for monitoring variable values or execution progress without interrupting the code with message boxes.

- **How to Use:** Insert **Debug.Print** in your code where you want to track variable values or execution flow.

- **Example:**

```
Sub CalculateTotal()
    Dim total As Double
    total = 100 * 0.05
    Debug.Print "Total calculated: " & total
End Sub
```

Using Breakpoints and Watch Windows

Breakpoints and **Watch Windows** are powerful debugging tools that allow you to control the execution of your code and monitor specific variables or expressions.

Breakpoints:

- **What They Are:** Breakpoints pause the execution of your code at a specified line, allowing you to inspect the state of your application at that point.

- **How to Set:** Click in the margin next to a line of code or press **F9** to toggle a breakpoint.

- **Using Breakpoints:**

  - **Step Through Code:** Once execution is paused at a breakpoint, you can step through your code line by line using **F8** to execute each line.

o   **Inspect Variables:** While paused, hover over variables to see their current values or use the Locals Window to inspect them.

Watch Windows:

- **What They Are:** Watch Windows allow you to monitor the value of specific variables or expressions as your code executes. You can set a watch to break execution when a certain condition is met.

- **How to Set:** Right-click a variable or expression in your code and select **Add Watch**, or go to **Debug > Add Watch**.

- **Types of Watches:**

    o   **Simple Watch:** Displays the current value of the variable or expression.

    o   **Break When Value Changes:** Pauses execution when the value of the variable changes.

    o   **Break When True:** Pauses execution when the expression evaluates to True.

- **Example:**

```
Sub MonitorValue()
    Dim x As Integer
    For x = 1 To 10
        Debug.Print x
    Next x
End Sub
```

- Set a watch on **x** to pause execution when **x = 5**.

Using breakpoints and watch windows effectively can significantly speed up the debugging process by allowing you to focus on the specific parts of your code that may be causing issues.

Error Handling Techniques: On Error Resume Next, On Error GoTo

Even with thorough testing and debugging, runtime errors can still occur. VBA provides several mechanisms to handle these errors gracefully, ensuring your code doesn't crash unexpectedly and providing users with meaningful feedback or alternative actions.

On Error Resume Next:

- **What It Does:** The On Error Resume Next statement tells VBA to continue executing the next line of code when a runtime error occurs, skipping the error.

- **When to Use:** Use On Error Resume Next sparingly, typically when you expect certain errors to occur and want to handle them directly in the code without interrupting execution.

- **Example:**

```
Sub SafeDivide()
    On Error Resume Next
    Dim result As Double
    result = 10 / 0 ' Runtime error, division by zero
    If Err.Number <> 0 Then
        MsgBox "An error occurred: " & Err.Description
        Err.Clear
    End If
End Sub
```

On Error GoTo:

- **What It Does:** The On Error GoTo statement directs VBA to jump to a specific line of code when an error occurs, allowing you to handle the error in a controlled manner.

- **When to Use:** Use On Error GoTo when you want to manage errors explicitly, such as logging them, showing custom error messages, or performing cleanup tasks.

- **Example:**

```
Sub ErrorHandlingExample()
    On Error GoTo ErrorHandler
    Dim ws As Worksheet
    Set ws = ThisWorkbook.Sheets("NonExistentSheet") '
Runtime error if sheet doesn't exist
    Exit Sub
```

```
ErrorHandler:
    MsgBox "An error occurred: " & Err.Description
    Err.Clear
End Sub
```

Error Handling Best Practices:

- **Clear Errors:** Always clear errors using **Err.Clear** after handling them to avoid unexpected behavior later in your code.

- **Provide Feedback:** When an error occurs, inform the user with a clear and helpful message, explaining what went wrong and, if possible, how to resolve it.

- **Exit Gracefully:** Ensure that your error handling allows the program to exit gracefully, even if an unexpected error occurs. This might involve closing open files, releasing resources, or resetting the application to a known state.

- **Use Error Handling for Critical Operations:** Apply error handling around critical operations such as file I/O, database access, or any code that interacts with external resources.

Combining Error Handling with Debugging:

- During development, you can temporarily disable error handling (**On Error GoTo 0**) to allow errors to halt the program, making them easier to debug. Once the code is tested, re-enable error handling to manage any errors that may occur in production.

Example of Comprehensive Error Handling:

```
Sub ComprehensiveErrorHandling()
    On Error GoTo ErrorHandler

    ' Code that may cause an error
    Dim wb As Workbook
    Set wb =
Workbooks.Open("C:\Path\To\NonExistentFile.xlsx")

    Exit Sub
```

```
ErrorHandler:
    MsgBox "An error occurred: " & Err.Description
    ' Perform any cleanup tasks here
    Err.Clear
End Sub
```

Writing Robust Code with Defensive Programming

In the realm of VBA programming, creating code that not only functions correctly but also withstands unexpected scenarios is paramount. **Defensive programming** is a methodology aimed at anticipating potential issues and implementing safeguards to ensure your code remains reliable and maintainable under various conditions. By adopting defensive programming practices, you can minimize bugs, enhance code readability, and improve overall application stability.

Key Principles of Defensive Programming:

1. **Input Validation:**

    o   **Why It Matters:** Ensuring that the data your code receives is valid prevents unexpected behavior and runtime errors.

    o   **How to Implement:** Before processing inputs, check for correct data types, ranges, and formats.

    o   **Example:**

```
Function GetUserAge(ageInput As String) As Integer
    If IsNumeric(ageInput) Then
        Dim age As Integer
        age = CInt(ageInput)
        If age > 0 And age < 120 Then
            GetUserAge = age
        Else
            MsgBox "Please enter a realistic
age.", vbExclamation
            GetUserAge = -1
        End If
    Else
```

```
        MsgBox "Age must be a number.",
vbExclamation
            GetUserAge = -1
        End If
    End Function
```

2. **Error Handling:**

- **Why It Matters:** Even with thorough validation, unforeseen errors can occur. Proper error handling ensures that your program can gracefully manage these situations without crashing.

- **How to Implement:** Use structured error handling (On Error GoTo) to catch and respond to errors appropriately.

- **Example:**

```
Sub OpenFileSafely(filePath As String)
    On Error GoTo ErrorHandler
    Dim wb As Workbook
    Set wb = Workbooks.Open(filePath)
    ' Proceed with operations on the workbook
    Exit Sub

ErrorHandler:
    MsgBox "Unable to open the file. Please check the file
path and try again.", vbCritical
    ' Additional cleanup if necessary
End Sub
```

3. **Clear and Maintainable Code:**

- **Why It Matters:** Writing clean, well-documented code makes it easier to understand, maintain, and debug, reducing the likelihood of introducing errors.

- **How to Implement:** Use meaningful variable names, comment your code, and adhere to consistent formatting standards.

- **Example:**

```
' Calculates the total sales for a given month
Function CalculateMonthlySales(month As String) As Double
```

```
        Dim totalSales As Double
        totalSales = 0
        ' Loop through sales records and accumulate totals
        ' [Insert loop logic here]
        CalculateMonthlySales = totalSales
End Function
```

4. **Assume the Unexpected:**

- **Why It Matters:** By anticipating that things can go wrong, you build resilience into your applications.

- **How to Implement:** Consider edge cases and handle scenarios where inputs or states might not be as expected.

- **Example:**

```
Sub ProcessData()
    If ThisWorkbook.Sheets.Count = 0 Then
        MsgBox "No worksheets found in the workbook.",
vbExclamation
        Exit Sub
    End If
    ' Proceed with data processing
End Sub
```

5. **Use Assertions:**

- **Why It Matters:** Assertions help verify that your code is functioning as intended during development.

- **How to Implement:** Use conditional checks to ensure that critical assumptions hold true.

```
Example:
Sub CalculateDiscount(price As Double, discountRate As
Double)
    ' Assert that discount rate is between 0 and 1
    If discountRate < 0 Or discountRate > 1 Then
        MsgBox "Discount rate must be between 0 and 1.",
vbCritical
        Exit Sub
```

```
        End If
        Dim discount As Double
        discount = price * discountRate
        MsgBox "Discount Amount: " & discount
    End Sub
```

Benefits of Defensive Programming:

- **Enhanced Reliability:** Reduces the likelihood of unexpected crashes and ensures your application behaves predictably.

- **Improved User Experience:** Users encounter fewer errors and receive clear messages when issues arise.

- **Easier Maintenance:** Clean and well-structured code is simpler to update and debug, facilitating long-term project sustainability.

- **Security:** Protects against invalid inputs that could potentially be exploited, safeguarding your application's integrity.

Conclusion

Debugging and error handling are critical skills in VBA programming, ensuring that your code is reliable, maintainable, and user-friendly. By understanding the different types of errors, using the VBA Editor's debugging tools, setting breakpoints, and applying effective error-handling techniques, you can develop robust Excel applications that handle unexpected situations gracefully. As you continue to refine your VBA skills, these practices will help you write cleaner, more efficient code, ultimately leading to more successful and resilient projects. In the following chapters, you will explore more advanced topics, including optimizing your VBA code for performance, integrating with other Office applications, and beyond.

Part III: Advanced VBA Techniques

9. Advanced Programming Techniques

As you advance in your VBA programming journey, you'll encounter scenarios where basic techniques may not be sufficient to handle complex tasks or large datasets. In this chapter, we'll explore advanced programming techniques in VBA, including working with arrays and collections, using dictionaries, creating custom classes, interacting with other Office applications, and accessing external data sources. These techniques will empower you to write more efficient, scalable, and sophisticated Excel applications.

Working with Arrays and Collections

Working with Arrays and Collections

Arrays and collections are powerful data structures that allow you to store and manipulate multiple values in a single variable. Understanding how to use these structures effectively can significantly enhance the performance and flexibility of your VBA code.

Arrays:

- **What They Are:** Arrays are variables that can hold multiple values, each identified by an index. Arrays can be one-dimensional (like a list) or multi-dimensional (like a table or matrix).

- **Declaring Arrays:** You declare an array using the **Dim** statement, specifying the number of elements it can hold.

    o **Example of a One-Dimensional Array:**

    ```
    Dim numbers(1 To 5) As Integer
    ```

    o **Example of a Multi-Dimensional Array:**

    ```
    Dim matrix(1 To 3, 1 To 3) As Double
    ```

- **Populating Arrays:**

    o You can populate arrays using loops or by directly assigning values.

    o **Example:**

```
Dim i As Integer
For i = 1 To 5
    numbers(i) = i * 10
Next i
```

- **Dynamic Arrays:**

  o Dynamic arrays can be resized during runtime using the **ReDim** statement.

  o **Example:**

  ```
  Dim scores() As Integer
  ReDim scores(1 To 10) ' Resize array to hold 10
  elements
  ```

- **Using Arrays in Functions:**

  o Arrays can be passed to and returned from functions, allowing you to process and return multiple values.

  o **Example:**

  ```
  Function GetMultiplesOfTen(ByVal n As Integer) As
  Integer()
      Dim multiples() As Integer
      ReDim multiples(1 To n)
      Dim i As Integer
      For i = 1 To n
          multiples(i) = i * 10
      Next i
      GetMultiplesOfTen = multiples
  End Function
  ```

Collections:

- **What They Are:** Collections are similar to arrays but are more flexible and easier to use. Unlike arrays, collections can grow or shrink dynamically, and you can add, remove, or reference items using keys.

- **Creating a Collection:**

  o **Example:**

  ```
  Dim students As New Collection
  ```

```
students.Add "Alice"
students.Add "Bob"
students.Add "Charlie"
```

- **Accessing Items in a Collection:**

  o You can access items in a collection using their index or a key.

  o **Example:**

  ```
  MsgBox students(1) ' Displays "Alice"
  ```

- **Using Keys with Collections:**

  o **Example:**

  ```
  students.Add "David", "D"
  MsgBox students("D") ' Displays "David"
  ```

- **Iterating Over Collections:**

  o Collections can be easily iterated using the For Each loop.

  o **Example:**

  ```
  Dim student As Variant
  For Each student In students
      MsgBox student
  Next student
  ```

When to Use Arrays vs. Collections:

- **Arrays:** Best for fixed-size datasets or when performance is critical.

- **Collections:** Best for dynamic datasets where the number of items may change or when you need to reference items by a key.

Using Dictionaries in VBA

The **Dictionary** object, part of the Microsoft Scripting Runtime library, offers a powerful alternative to collections, providing fast lookups, unique keys, and the ability to store key-value pairs.

Creating and Using a Dictionary:

- **Setting Up:** You need to enable the "Microsoft Scripting Runtime" reference in your VBA project to use dictionaries.

- o **Example:**

```
Dim dict As Object
Set dict = CreateObject("Scripting.Dictionary")
```

- • **Adding Items to a Dictionary:**

  - o Dictionaries store data in key-value pairs.

  - o **Example:**

```
dict.Add "A001", "Alice"
dict.Add "B002", "Bob"
```

- • **Accessing Dictionary Items:**

  - o You can access values by referencing their keys.

  - o **Example:**

```
MsgBox dict("A001") ' Displays "Alice"
```

- • **Checking for Key Existence:**

  - o **Example:**

```
If dict.Exists("A001") Then
    MsgBox "Key exists!"
Else
    MsgBox "Key does not exist."
End If
```

- • **Removing Items:**

  - o **Example:**

```
dict.Remove "A001"
```

- • **Iterating Through a Dictionary:**

  - o **Example:**

```
Dim key As Variant
For Each key In dict.Keys
    MsgBox key & ": " & dict(key)
Next key
```

Advantages of Using Dictionaries:

- **Fast Lookups:** Dictionary lookups are generally faster than searching through arrays or collections.

- **Unique Keys:** Ensures that each key is unique, preventing duplicate entries.

- **Dynamic Sizing:** Like collections, dictionaries grow or shrink dynamically.

Dictionaries are particularly useful when you need to associate unique keys with specific values and perform quick lookups or when managing large datasets where performance is a concern.

Creating and Using Custom Classes

Custom classes allow you to encapsulate data and functionality into objects, making your code more modular, reusable, and easier to maintain.

What is a Class?

- A class is a blueprint for an object. It defines the properties (data) and methods (functions or procedures) that the object will have.

- In VBA, classes are defined using **Class Modules**.

Creating a Custom Class:

1. **Insert a Class Module:**

    - In the VBA Editor, go to **Insert > Class Module**. A new class module will appear in the Project Explorer.

    - Rename the class module to something meaningful, like **clsEmployee**.

2. **Defining Properties:**

    - Properties store data related to the object. You define them using **Public** variables or using **Property Let**, **Property Get**, and **Property Set** procedures for more control.

    - **Example:**

    ```
    ' Inside clsEmployee class module
    Private pName As String
    Private pID As String
    ```

```
Public Property Let Name(value As String)
    pName = value
End Property

Public Property Get Name() As String
    Name = pName
End Property

Public Property Let ID(value As String)
    pID = value
End Property

Public Property Get ID() As String
    ID = pID
End Property
```

3. **Defining Methods:**

- Methods are functions or procedures that belong to the class and operate on its properties.

- **Example:**

```
Public Sub DisplayInfo()
    MsgBox "Employee Name: " & Name & vbCrLf &
    "Employee ID: " & ID
End Sub
```

4. **Using the Custom Class:**

- Once the class is defined, you can create instances of it and use its properties and methods.

- **Example:**

```
Sub TestEmployeeClass()
    Dim emp As clsEmployee
    Set emp = New clsEmployee
    emp.Name = "John Doe"
    emp.ID = "E123"
```

```
        emp.DisplayInfo
    End Sub
```

Benefits of Using Classes:

- **Encapsulation:** Keeps related data and functionality together, improving code organization.

- **Reusability:** Once a class is created, it can be reused throughout your application or even in other projects.

- **Maintainability:** Changes to a class can be made in one place, without affecting the rest of your code.

Real-World Applications of Custom Classes:

- Modeling real-world entities like employees, products, or transactions.

- Creating complex objects that require multiple properties and methods.

- Building frameworks or libraries that can be easily adapted and extended.

Interacting with Other Office Applications: Word, Outlook, and PowerPoint

VBA allows you to control other Microsoft Office applications directly from Excel, enabling you to automate tasks across different platforms.

Controlling Word from Excel:

- You can automate Word to create documents, insert text, format content, and more.

- **Example:**

```
Sub CreateWordDocument()
    Dim wdApp As Object
    Dim wdDoc As Object
    Set wdApp = CreateObject("Word.Application")
    Set wdDoc = wdApp.Documents.Add
    wdApp.Visible = True
```

```
With wdDoc
        .Content.Text = "This is a test document created
from Excel VBA."
        .SaveAs "C:\Path\To\Document.docx"
    End With

    wdApp.Quit
End Sub
```

Controlling Outlook from Excel:

- You can automate Outlook to send emails, manage appointments, and handle contacts.

- **Example:**

```
Sub SendEmail()
    Dim olApp As Object
    Dim olMail As Object
    Set olApp = CreateObject("Outlook.Application")
    Set olMail = olApp.CreateItem(0)

    With olMail
        .To = "recipient@example.com"
        .Subject = "Test Email"
        .Body = "This email was sent using Excel VBA."
        .Send
    End With
End Sub
```

Controlling PowerPoint from Excel:

- You can automate PowerPoint to create presentations, add slides, and insert content.

- **Example:**

```
Sub CreatePowerPointPresentation()
    Dim pptApp As Object
    Dim pptPres As Object
```

```
Dim slide As Object
Set pptApp = CreateObject("PowerPoint.Application")
Set pptPres = pptApp.Presentations.Add
pptApp.Visible = True

Set slide = pptPres.Slides.Add(1, 1)
slide.Shapes.Title.TextFrame.TextRange.Text = "VBA
Automation"
slide.Shapes.Placeholders(2).TextFrame.TextRange.Text
= "Created from Excel VBA"

pptPres.SaveAs "C:\Path\To\Presentation.pptx"
pptApp.Quit
End Sub
```

Advantages of Interacting with Other Office Applications:

- **Efficiency:** Automate repetitive tasks that involve multiple applications.

- **Consistency:** Ensure consistent formatting, content, and structure across different documents.

- **Integration:** Build integrated solutions that leverage the strengths of different Office applications.

Accessing External Data Sources: Databases and Web Services

VBA can interact with external data sources, such as databases and web services, allowing you to pull in data, perform operations, and update records directly from Excel.

Connecting to Databases:

- You can use ADO (ActiveX Data Objects) to connect to and interact with databases like Access, SQL Server, or Oracle.

- **Example:**

```
Sub GetDataFromDatabase()
```

```vba
    Dim conn As Object
    Dim rs As Object
    Dim connectionString As String
    Dim sql As String

    connectionString =
"Provider=Microsoft.ACE.OLEDB.12.0;Data
Source=C:\Path\To\Database.accdb;"
    sql = "SELECT * FROM TableName"

    Set conn = CreateObject("ADODB.Connection")
    conn.Open connectionString

    Set rs = CreateObject("ADODB.Recordset")
    rs.Open sql, conn

    Do Until rs.EOF
        Debug.Print rs.Fields(0).Value ' Print the first
field of each record
        rs.MoveNext
    Loop

    rs.Close
    conn.Close
End Sub
```

Interacting with Web Services:

- You can use VBA to make HTTP requests and interact with web services, allowing your application to retrieve or send data over the internet.

- **Example:**

```vba
Sub GetDataFromWebService()
    Dim xmlHttp As Object
    Dim url As String
    url = "https://api.example.com/data"
```

```
Set xmlHttp = CreateObject("MSXML2.XMLHTTP")
xmlHttp.Open "GET", url, False
xmlHttp.send

If xmlHttp.Status = 200 Then
    Debug.Print xmlHttp.responseText
Else
    MsgBox "Request failed with status: " &
xmlHttp.Status
    End If
End Sub
```

Advantages of Accessing External Data Sources:

- **Data Integration:** Seamlessly integrate external data into your Excel workflows.

- **Automation:** Automate data retrieval and updates, reducing the need for manual data entry.

- **Enhanced Functionality:** Extend the capabilities of your Excel applications by leveraging external data sources.

By mastering the advanced programming techniques covered in this chapter, you can significantly enhance the capabilities of your VBA applications. Whether you're managing complex datasets with arrays and collections, creating custom objects with classes, integrating with other Office applications, or accessing external data sources, these skills will empower you to build sophisticated and scalable Excel solutions. In the next chapters, you'll continue to explore even more advanced topics, optimizing your code for performance, and beyond.

10. Optimizing VBA Code for Performance

As you develop more complex Excel applications using VBA, optimizing your code for performance becomes increasingly important. Slow or inefficient code can lead to long processing times, unresponsive workbooks, and frustrated users. In this chapter, we'll explore various strategies for optimizing VBA code, including identifying and addressing performance bottlenecks, implementing best practices for efficient coding, reducing calculation time, managing large datasets, and handling memory usage effectively.

Understanding VBA Performance Bottlenecks

Before diving into specific optimization techniques, it's crucial to understand the common sources of performance bottlenecks in VBA. Identifying these bottlenecks is the first step in improving your code's efficiency.

Common Performance Bottlenecks:

1. **Frequent Interaction with the Excel Object Model:**

    *   VBA frequently interacts with Excel's object model to manipulate workbooks, worksheets, ranges, and cells. Each interaction with the Excel interface can be slow, especially when performed repeatedly in loops.

    *   **Example:** Looping through cells individually to apply formatting or perform calculations.

2. **Unnecessary Recalculation:**

    *   Excel automatically recalculates formulas whenever a change is made to the workbook. This can be a significant performance drain, especially in large workbooks with many formulas.

    *   **Example:** Making changes to cells that trigger recalculations in a large number of dependent formulas.

3. **Inefficient Loops:**

    *   Poorly structured loops, such as looping through a large range of cells one by one, can severely impact performance.

    *   **Example:** A loop that processes thousands of cells individually rather than as a batch.

4. **Screen Updating:**

- VBA updates the Excel screen with every change made to the workbook. While this is useful for the user to see progress, it can slow down code execution.

- **Example:** Real-time screen updates while populating large ranges.

5. **Excessive Use of Volatile Functions:**

- Volatile functions like **NOW()**, **RAND()**, and **OFFSET()** recalculate every time any change is made in the workbook, which can lead to performance issues.

- **Example:** Using **NOW()** in multiple cells across a large worksheet.

Identifying Bottlenecks:

- Use VBA's built-in debugging tools to identify which parts of your code are taking the most time to execute. The **Timer** function can be particularly useful for measuring the time taken by specific sections of code.

- **Example:**

```
Sub MeasurePerformance()
    Dim startTime As Double
    Dim endTime As Double

    startTime = Timer
    ' Code to measure goes here
    endTime = Timer

    MsgBox "Time taken: " & (endTime - startTime) & "
seconds"
End Sub
```

Understanding where your code is slowing down allows you to target optimizations more effectively.

Writing Efficient Code: Best Practices

Writing efficient VBA code involves following best practices that minimize unnecessary operations, reduce interaction with the Excel object model, and streamline your code.

Best Practices for Writing Efficient VBA Code:

1. **Minimize Interactions with Excel Objects:**

   - Reduce the number of times your code interacts with Excel objects by batching operations or working with arrays.

   - **Example:** Instead of writing data to cells one by one, write all data at once using an array.

   ```
   Sub BatchWriteData()
       Dim data(1 To 100, 1 To 10) As Variant
       ' Populate the array with data
       Dim i As Integer, j As Integer
       For i = 1 To 100
           For j = 1 To 10
               data(i, j) = i * j
           Next j
       Next i


       ' Write the entire array to the worksheet in one go

       ThisWorkbook.Sheets("Sheet1").Range("A1:J100").Value
       = data
   End Sub
   ```

2. **Disable Screen Updating:**

   - Turn off screen updating during code execution to prevent Excel from redrawing the screen with every change.
   - **Example:**

   ```
   Sub OptimizeScreenUpdating()
       Application.ScreenUpdating = False
       ' Your code here
   ```

```
        Application.ScreenUpdating = True
    End Sub
```

3. **Turn Off Automatic Calculations Temporarily:**

   - Temporarily set Excel's calculation mode to manual to prevent unnecessary recalculations during code execution.

   - **Example:**

```
Sub OptimizeCalculations()
    Application.Calculation = xlCalculationManual
    ' Your code here
    Application.Calculation = xlCalculationAutomatic
    Application.Calculate ' Force recalculation if
needed
End Sub
```

4. **Avoid Using Select and Activate:**

   - Avoid unnecessary use of Select and Activate to reference ranges or sheets. Instead, directly reference objects.

   - **Example:**

```
' Instead of this:
Sheets("Sheet1").Select
Range("A1").Select
ActiveCell.Value = "Hello"


' Do this:
Sheets("Sheet1").Range("A1").Value = "Hello"
```

5. **Use With Statements:**

   - Use With statements to reduce repetitive object references, making your code cleaner and faster.

   - **Example:**

```
With Sheets("Sheet1")
        .Range("A1").Value = "Name"
        .Range("B1").Value = "Age"
        .Range("C1").Value = "Location"
```

```
End With
```

6. **Optimize Loops:**

- Avoid looping through large ranges if possible. Instead, work with arrays or use Excel's built-in functions.

- **Example:** Using Application.WorksheetFunction to perform bulk operations instead of looping.

```
Sub OptimizeLoop()
    Dim rng As Range
    Set rng = Sheets("Sheet1").Range("A1:A1000")
    rng.Value =
Application.WorksheetFunction.Transpose(Sheets("Sheet2
").Range("B1:B1000"))
End Sub
```

By following these best practices, you can significantly improve the efficiency of your VBA code, making it run faster and more smoothly.

Reducing Workbook and Worksheet Calculation Time

Calculation time in Excel can be a significant bottleneck, especially in workbooks with complex formulas, large datasets, or numerous volatile functions. Optimizing calculation processes can greatly enhance performance.

Strategies to Reduce Calculation Time:

1. **Minimize the Use of Volatile Functions:**

- Volatile functions recalculate every time a change is made, which can slow down your workbook. Replace volatile functions with static equivalents where possible.

- **Example:** Replace **NOW()** with a static timestamp using **Ctrl + Shift + ;**.

2. **Use Manual Calculation Mode:**

- Set Excel to manual calculation mode while running VBA code to prevent recalculations until necessary.

- **Example:**

```
Sub ManualCalculationMode()
```

```
Application.Calculation = xlCalculationManual
' Your code here
Application.Calculation = xlCalculationAutomatic
Application.Calculate
End Sub
```

3. **Limit the Calculation Scope:**

    - Reduce the calculation scope by referencing only the necessary ranges rather than entire columns or sheets.

    - **Example:** Instead of using formulas on entire columns (**A:A**), limit the range to just the rows needed (**A1:A100**).

4. **Use Efficient Formulas:**

    - Simplify formulas to reduce calculation time. Avoid unnecessary array formulas and use helper columns where appropriate.

    - **Example:** Replace complex nested formulas with simpler, sequential calculations.

5. **Optimize Data Tables and PivotTables:**

    - Reduce the size of data tables and PivotTables by filtering out unnecessary data and using only the columns required for calculations.

By implementing these strategies, you can significantly reduce the time Excel spends on calculations, making your workbook more responsive.

Working with Large Datasets

Handling large datasets efficiently is crucial when working with VBA, as processing large amounts of data can quickly slow down your application. Here are some techniques for optimizing your code when working with large datasets.

Techniques for Handling Large Datasets:

1. **Work with Arrays Instead of Ranges:**

    - Load data into an array, process the data in memory, and then write the results back to the worksheet. This minimizes interaction with the Excel object model.

- **Example:**

```
Sub ProcessLargeDataset()
    Dim data As Variant
    Dim i As Long

    ' Load data into array
    data = Sheets("Sheet1").Range("A1:A10000").Value

    ' Process data in array
    For i = 1 To UBound(data)
        data(i, 1) = data(i, 1) * 2
    Next i

    ' Write processed data back to sheet
    Sheets("Sheet1").Range("B1:B10000").Value = data
End Sub
```

2. **Use Database Techniques:**

   - Treat large datasets as databases by using SQL queries within Excel (via ADO) or by leveraging PivotTables for summarizing data.

   - **Example:** Use **Application.WorksheetFunction** for operations like **SUMIF**, **COUNTIF**, or **VLOOKUP** instead of looping through large ranges.

3. **Filter Data Early:**

   - Filter and reduce the dataset size before performing operations. This reduces the number of iterations or calculations required.

   - **Example:** Apply an auto filter to the dataset and process only the visible rows.

4. **Limit the Use of Worksheet Functions in VBA:**

   - Worksheet functions are convenient but can be slower than equivalent VBA code, especially when used in loops. Use VBA's built-in functions or algorithms where possible.

- **Example:** Instead of using Application.WorksheetFunction.Sum, sum values directly in VBA:

```
Dim total As Double
For i = 1 To 10000
    total = total + Cells(i, 1).Value
Next i
```

5. **Efficient Data Sorting and Searching:**

- Use VBA's **Sort** method or leverage arrays and dictionaries for efficient searching and sorting operations on large datasets.

By optimizing how your code handles large datasets, you can significantly improve performance, allowing your VBA applications to handle more data without slowing down.

Memory Management in VBA

Efficient memory management is essential in VBA, particularly when dealing with large datasets, complex calculations, or multiple objects. Poor memory management can lead to slower performance, memory leaks, or even crashes.

Strategies for Managing Memory in VBA:

1. **Release Object References:**

- Always release object references when they are no longer needed to free up memory.

- **Example:**

```
Sub CleanUp()
    Dim wb As Workbook
    Set wb = Workbooks.Open("C:\Path\To\File.xlsx")
    ' Work with the workbook
    Set wb = Nothing ' Release the object reference
End Sub
```

2. **Use Erase to Clear Arrays:**

- If you have used a large array, use the Erase statement to free up the memory it occupied.

- **Example:**

```
Dim data() As Variant
' Code that uses the array
Erase data ' Clear the array from memory
```

3. **Avoid Unnecessary Variable Declarations:**

   - Declare only the variables you need and reuse variables where appropriate to minimize memory usage.

   - **Example:** Reuse loop counters or other temporary variables when possible.

4. **Avoid Excessive Use of Variants:**

   - Variant data types consume more memory than other types like Integer or Double. Use specific data types where possible.

   - **Example:**

   ```
   ' Instead of this:
   Dim num As Variant
   num = 10


   ' Do this:
   Dim num As Integer
   num = 10
   ```

5. **Limit the Use of Global Variables:**

   - Global variables remain in memory for the duration of the workbook session. Use them sparingly and consider local variables or passing arguments between procedures instead.

   - **Example:** Pass data between procedures using arguments rather than relying on global variables.

6. **Optimize UserForm and Control Usage:**

   - If your application uses UserForms, consider unloading forms when they are no longer needed to free up memory.

   - **Example:**

   ```
   Unload UserForm1
   ```

Memory Leaks and Prevention:

- A memory leak occurs when memory that is no longer needed is not released, gradually reducing the amount of available memory. Properly releasing objects, clearing arrays, and minimizing the use of global variables can help prevent memory leaks.

By managing memory effectively, you can ensure that your VBA applications remain responsive and stable, even when dealing with large datasets or complex operations.

In this chapter, you've learned essential techniques for optimizing VBA code for performance. By understanding and addressing performance bottlenecks, following best practices for writing efficient code, reducing calculation time, handling large datasets effectively, and managing memory usage, you can significantly improve the performance of your Excel applications. These optimizations not only make your code run faster but also enhance the overall user experience, ensuring that your applications are both powerful and efficient. As you continue to build more advanced solutions in VBA, these techniques will be invaluable in maintaining high performance and reliability.

11. Creating Custom Functions and Add-Ins

Creating custom functions and add-ins in Excel allows you to extend the functionality of the application, providing powerful tools that can be reused across multiple workbooks and shared with others. In this chapter, you will learn how to write custom worksheet functions, create and distribute Excel add-ins, manage versions and updates, and protect your code with password protection and digital signatures. By mastering these techniques, you can create robust, reusable solutions that enhance productivity and streamline workflows.

Writing Custom Worksheet Functions

Writing Custom Worksheet Functions

Custom functions, also known as **User-Defined Functions (UDFs)**, allow you to create specialized calculations that go beyond Excel's built-in functions. These functions can be used directly in worksheet formulas just like native Excel functions.

Creating a Simple Custom Function:

- Custom functions are written in VBA and placed in a standard module. The **Function** keyword is used to define a UDF.

- **Example:**

  ```
  Function AddNumbers(ByVal num1 As Double, ByVal num2 As
  Double) As Double
      AddNumbers = num1 + num2
  End Function
  ```

- Usage in Excel: **=AddNumbers(5, 10)**, which returns **15**.

Returning Complex Data Types:

- UDFs can return more than just numbers or text. You can return arrays or even error values to handle specific scenarios.

- **Example of Returning an Array:**

  ```
  Function MultiplyRange(rng As Range, factor As Double) As
  Variant
      Dim result() As Double
  ```

```
    Dim i As Integer
    ReDim result(1 To rng.Cells.Count)

    For i = 1 To rng.Cells.Count
        result(i) = rng.Cells(i).Value * factor
    Next i

    MultiplyRange =
Application.WorksheetFunction.Transpose(result)
End Function
```

- Usage in Excel: Select a vertical range, enter **=MultiplyRange(A1:A5, 2)** and press **Ctrl + Shift + Enter** for an array formula.

Handling Errors in Custom Functions:

- To make your UDFs more robust, handle potential errors gracefully by returning error values that Excel can interpret, like **#DIV/0!** or **#N/A**.

- **Example:**

```
Function SafeDivide(ByVal numerator As Double, ByVal
denominator As Double) As Variant
    If denominator = 0 Then
        SafeDivide = CVErr(xlErrDiv0)
    Else
        SafeDivide = numerator / denominator
    End If
End Function
```

- Usage in Excel: **=SafeDivide(10, 0)** returns **#DIV/0!**.

Making Functions Volatile:

- By default, custom functions only recalculate when their input values change. However, you can make them volatile, meaning they recalculate every time any cell in the worksheet recalculates.

- **Example:**

```
Function CurrentTime() As String
    Application.Volatile
```

```
CurrentTime = Format(Now, "hh:mm:ss AM/PM")
End Function
```

- Usage in Excel: **=CurrentTime()**, which updates every time the sheet recalculates.

Custom functions are an excellent way to encapsulate complex logic into reusable formulas, making your spreadsheets more powerful and tailored to specific tasks.

Creating Add-Ins in Excel

An Excel add-in is a type of workbook that provides additional functionality in Excel. By creating an add-in, you can package your custom functions, macros, and tools into a single file that can be easily distributed and installed by others.

Steps to Create an Add-In:

1. **Develop Your VBA Code:**

   - Write all the necessary functions, macros, and procedures in a standard workbook. Ensure that your code is well-organized, with clear comments and modular functions.

2. **Save the Workbook as an Add-In:**

   - Go to **File > Save As**.

   - In the "Save as type" dropdown, select **Excel Add-In (*.xlam)**.

   - Save the file with a descriptive name.

3. **Load the Add-In:**

   - After saving, load the add-in into Excel to test it.

   - Go to **File > Options > Add-Ins**.

   - In the "Manage" dropdown, select **Excel Add-ins** and click **Go**.

   - Click **Browse** to find and select your **.xlam** file.

   - Ensure your add-in is checked in the list to activate it.

Customizing the Add-In:

- **Adding a Custom Ribbon Tab:** You can enhance your add-in by creating a custom Ribbon tab with buttons for your macros and functions.

- **Example:**

  o Use the **RibbonX** XML in combination with VBA to create custom tabs and controls. This allows you to design a user-friendly interface for your add-in.

Example of a Simple Add-In with a Macro:

```
Sub HighlightDuplicates()
    Dim rng As Range
    Set rng = Selection
    rng.FormatConditions.AddUniqueValues

    rng.FormatConditions(rng.FormatConditions.Count).SetFirstP
riority
        With rng.FormatConditions(1).Font
            .Color = -16776961
            .TintAndShade = 0
        End With
        rng.FormatConditions(1).DupeUnique = xlDuplicate
End Sub
```

- This macro highlights duplicate values in the selected range. Once packaged in an add-in, it can be executed from a custom button on the Ribbon.

Add-ins are a powerful way to package and distribute your VBA solutions, making them easily accessible across different workbooks and by different users.

Distributing and Installing Add-Ins

Distributing and Installing Add-Ins

Once your add-in is created, you'll want to distribute it to others and ensure it can be easily installed. There are several methods to distribute and install Excel add-ins.

Distributing Add-Ins:

1. **Via Email or Shared Drive:**

   - Share the **.xlam** file directly via email or a shared network drive. Users can then download and install the add-in manually.

2. **Using a Shared Network Location:**

   - Store the add-in on a shared network location. Users can install the add-in from this location, ensuring everyone has access to the same version.

3. **Online Distribution:**

   - Host the add-in on a website or cloud storage service. Provide users with a link to download and install the add-in.

Installing Add-Ins:

1. **Manual Installation:**

   - After receiving the add-in file, users can install it by going to **File > Options > Add-Ins**, selecting **Excel Add-ins**, and browsing to the add-in file.

2. **Automating the Installation:**

   - You can create a simple installation script or provide detailed instructions to help users install the add-in without needing to navigate Excel's settings.

3. **Adding to Startup:**

   - To ensure the add-in loads every time Excel starts, users can place the add-in file in Excel's startup folder (**C:\Users\[YourUsername]\AppData\Roaming\Microsoft\Excel \XLSTART**).

Ensuring Compatibility:

- When distributing your add-in, make sure it's compatible with the versions of Excel that your users have. Testing across different versions can prevent issues related to deprecated features or changes in the object model.

Distributing your add-ins efficiently ensures that your tools are accessible to a wide audience and can be easily installed and used.

Managing Versions and Updates for Add-Ins

As you improve your add-ins or fix bugs, you may need to release new versions. Managing these versions and ensuring users can easily update their add-ins is crucial.

Version Control:

1. **Version Numbering:**

   - Implement a version numbering system (e.g., 1.0, 1.1, 2.0) to keep track of changes and updates.

   - **Example:**

     ```
     Public Const VersionNumber As String = "1.2"
     ```

2. **Change Logs:**

   - Maintain a change log that documents what has been added, changed, or fixed in each version. This log can be included in the add-in itself or distributed alongside it.

3. **Backward Compatibility:**

   - Ensure that updates do not break existing functionality. Test new versions thoroughly to maintain compatibility with older versions.

Updating Add-Ins:

1. **Automated Updates:**

   - Consider implementing a version check in your add-in. When the add-in loads, it could check for a newer version and prompt the user to download the update.

   - **Example:**

     ```
     Sub CheckForUpdates()
         Dim latestVersion As String
         ' Assume a function that retrieves the latest
     version from a server
         latestVersion = GetLatestVersionFromServer()

         If latestVersion > VersionNumber Then
     ```

```
        MsgBox "A new version of the add-in is
    available. Please update.", vbInformation
                ' Optionally provide a link to download the
        new version
            End If
        End Sub
```

2. **Manual Updates:**

   - Notify users of updates via email or a notification within the add-in. Provide them with instructions on how to download and install the latest version.

3. **Rolling Back:**

   - Keep older versions of your add-in available so users can roll back if necessary. This is particularly important if a new version introduces unexpected issues.

Effective version management ensures that your users always have access to the latest features and improvements while maintaining the stability of your add-ins.

Protecting Your Code: Password Protection and Digital Signatures

Protecting your VBA code from unauthorized access or modification is important, especially if your add-in contains proprietary logic or sensitive information.

Password Protecting Your VBA Code:

1. **Adding a Password to the VBA Project:**

   - In the VBA Editor, go to **Tools > VBAProject Properties**.

   - Under the "Protection" tab, check "Lock project for viewing" and set a password.

   - This prevents others from viewing or modifying your VBA code without the password.

2. **Considerations:**

- Be aware that password protection in VBA is not foolproof and can be bypassed with specialized tools. However, it does provide a basic level of security.

- Always keep a secure copy of your password in case you need to access the code later.

Using Digital Signatures:

1. **What Are Digital Signatures?**

   - A digital signature certifies the authenticity of your code and ensures that it hasn't been altered since it was signed. This is important for maintaining trust and security, especially when distributing add-ins to a wide audience.

2. **Creating a Digital Signature:**

   - You can create a digital certificate using tools like SelfCert (included with Office) or obtain a certificate from a trusted certificate authority (CA).

   - **Steps to Sign Your VBA Project:**

     o In the VBA Editor, go to **Tools** > **Digital Signature**.

     o Select your certificate and apply it to the project.

3. **Benefits of Digital Signatures:**

   - A signed VBA project is less likely to be flagged by security software, and users can be assured that the code comes from a trusted source.

   - If the code is altered after signing, the signature is invalidated, alerting users to potential tampering.

4. **Managing Certificates:**

   - If using a self-signed certificate, remember that it may not be trusted by all users or on all systems. Using a certificate from a CA is more secure but involves additional cost and setup.

Conclusion:

Protecting your VBA code is crucial for maintaining the integrity and security of your add-ins, especially when distributing them to others. Password protection provides basic security, while digital signatures offer a higher level of trust and assurance.

In this chapter, you have learned how to create custom functions and add-ins in Excel, distribute and manage them effectively, and protect your code from unauthorized access. These skills allow you to extend Excel's functionality, create reusable tools, and share them with others in a secure and professional manner. As you continue to develop more advanced Excel applications, these techniques will enable you to build robust, user-friendly, and secure solutions that can be widely adopted and easily maintained.

Part IV: Solving Real-World Problems with VBA and Macros

12. Automating Financial Models

In the world of finance, Excel is an indispensable tool for building, analyzing, and reporting financial models. By leveraging VBA and macros, you can automate these processes, making your financial models more dynamic, efficient, and error-resistant. This chapter will guide you through automating various aspects of financial modeling, from building dynamic models and automating financial analysis to creating custom financial reports. We'll also walk through a case study to demonstrate the practical application of these techniques in developing an automated budgeting tool.

Building Dynamic Financial Models

Building Dynamic Financial Models

Dynamic financial models are flexible tools that automatically update when assumptions, inputs, or data change. VBA can enhance these models by automating the process of updating inputs, recalculating projections, and ensuring that the model remains consistent and error-free.

Creating Dynamic Inputs:

- **Automated Input Updates:** Use VBA to pull in financial data from external sources, such as databases or web services, to ensure your model always uses the latest information.

  - **Example:**

    ```
    Sub UpdateExchangeRates()
        Dim ws As Worksheet
        Set ws = ThisWorkbook.Sheets("Assumptions")

        ' Assuming we have a web service that provides
    exchange rates
        ws.Range("B2").Value = GetExchangeRate("USD",
    "EUR") ' Custom function to get the rate
    ```

```
        ws.Range("B3").Value = GetExchangeRate("USD",
    "GBP")
    End Sub
```

- **Dynamic Ranges:** Use dynamic named ranges to automatically adjust the range of data used in your calculations when new data is added.

    o **Example:**

```
    Sub CreateDynamicNamedRange()
        Dim ws As Worksheet
        Set ws = ThisWorkbook.Sheets("Data")

        ws.Names.Add Name:="RevenueData",
    RefersTo:="=OFFSET(Data!$A$1,0,0,COUNTA(Data!$A:$A
    ),1)"
    End Sub
```

Automating Projections and Scenarios:

- **Scenario Analysis:** VBA can automate scenario analysis by quickly generating different financial outcomes based on varying assumptions.

    o **Example:**

```
    Sub RunScenarioAnalysis()
        Dim ws As Worksheet
        Set ws = ThisWorkbook.Sheets("Scenarios")

        ' Example scenarios
        ws.Range("B2").Value = 1.05 ' Growth Rate -
    Scenario 1
        ws.Range("C2").Value = 1.10 ' Growth Rate -
    Scenario 2
        ws.Range("D2").Value = 1.15 ' Growth Rate -
    Scenario 3

        Call UpdateFinancialModel ' Call a procedure
    to update the model based on new assumptions
    End Sub
```

- **Sensitivity Analysis:** Automate sensitivity analysis to see how changes in key inputs (e.g., discount rate, growth rate) affect the output.

    o **Example:**

    ```
    Sub RunSensitivityAnalysis()
        Dim ws As Worksheet
        Set ws = ThisWorkbook.Sheets("Sensitivity")

        Dim rate As Double
        For rate = 0.01 To 0.05 Step 0.01
            ws.Cells(1, rate * 100).Value = rate
            ws.Cells(2, rate * 100).Value =
    CalculateNPV(rate) ' Custom NPV function
        Next rate
    End Sub
    ```

Building Dynamic Financial Statements:

- **Automated Consolidation:** If your financial model includes multiple subsidiaries or business units, you can use VBA to consolidate their financial statements into a single model.

    o **Example:**

    ```
    Sub ConsolidateFinancials()
        Dim ws As Worksheet
        Set ws = ThisWorkbook.Sheets("Consolidated")

        ws.Range("B2").Value =
    Sheets("Subsidiary1").Range("B2").Value +
    Sheets("Subsidiary2").Range("B2").Value
        ws.Range("B3").Value =
    Sheets("Subsidiary1").Range("B3").Value +
    Sheets("Subsidiary2").Range("B3").Value
        ' Continue consolidating other line items
    End Sub
    ```

- **Automated Linking:** Use VBA to create dynamic links between your financial statements (Income Statement, Balance Sheet, Cash Flow Statement) to ensure they update automatically as inputs change.

  - **Example:**

    ```
    Sub LinkFinancialStatements()
        Dim incomeSheet As Worksheet
        Dim balanceSheet As Worksheet
        Set incomeSheet = ThisWorkbook.Sheets("Income
    Statement")
        Set balanceSheet =
    ThisWorkbook.Sheets("Balance Sheet")

        balanceSheet.Range("B10").Value =
    incomeSheet.Range("B20").Value ' Link Net Income
    to Retained Earnings
    End Sub
    ```

Building dynamic financial models with VBA enables you to create flexible and responsive tools that adapt to changes in inputs and assumptions, allowing for more accurate and efficient financial planning and analysis.

Automating Financial Analysis

Automating Financial Analysis

Automating financial analysis with VBA allows you to streamline repetitive tasks, reduce errors, and focus more on interpreting results rather than performing manual calculations.

Automating Ratio Analysis:

- **Calculating Financial Ratios:** Use VBA to automate the calculation of key financial ratios, such as profitability, liquidity, and leverage ratios.

  - **Example:**

    ```
    Sub CalculateFinancialRatios()
        Dim ws As Worksheet
        Set ws = ThisWorkbook.Sheets("Ratios")
    ```

```
    ws.Range("B2").Value = CalculateGrossMargin()
' Custom function to calculate Gross Margin
    ws.Range("B3").Value = CalculateCurrentRatio()
' Custom function to calculate Current Ratio
    ws.Range("B4").Value = CalculateDebtToEquity()
' Custom function to calculate Debt to Equity
Ratio
End Sub
```

- **Trend Analysis:** Automate trend analysis by calculating and visualizing the change in financial ratios over time.

  o **Example:**

```
Sub GenerateTrendAnalysis()
    Dim ws As Worksheet
    Set ws = ThisWorkbook.Sheets("Trends")

    ' Assuming financial ratios are stored in a
named range "RatioData"
    ws.Range("A1:A10").Value =
Application.WorksheetFunction.Trend(Range("RatioDa
ta"))
End Sub
```

Automating Valuation Models:

- **Discounted Cash Flow (DCF) Analysis:** Use VBA to automate DCF calculations, including the determination of free cash flows, discount rates, and terminal values.

  o **Example:**

```
Sub CalculateDCF()
    Dim ws As Worksheet
    Set ws = ThisWorkbook.Sheets("DCF")

    Dim cashFlows() As Double
    cashFlows = ws.Range("B2:B6").Value ' Assuming
free cash flows are stored here
```

```
ws.Range("B8").Value = CalculateNPV(cashFlows,
0.10) ' Custom NPV function with 10% discount rate
End Sub
```

- **Comparable Company Analysis:** Automate the process of retrieving and calculating valuation multiples from comparable companies.

  o **Example:**

```
Sub ComparableCompanyAnalysis()
    Dim ws As Worksheet
    Set ws = ThisWorkbook.Sheets("Comps")

    ' Assuming data is pulled into "Price",
"Earnings", etc.
    ws.Range("B2").Value = ws.Range("Price").Value
/ ws.Range("Earnings").Value ' P/E Ratio
    ws.Range("C2").Value = ws.Range("Price").Value
/ ws.Range("Sales").Value ' P/S Ratio
End Sub
```

Automating financial analysis with VBA enhances the accuracy and speed of your analysis, freeing up time to focus on strategic decision-making.

Creating Custom Financial Reports

Custom financial reports tailored to specific audiences or needs can be efficiently generated using VBA. Automating report creation ensures consistency and reduces the time required to produce these reports regularly.

Automating Report Generation:

- **Generating Standard Financial Reports:** Use VBA to automate the generation of standard financial reports such as income statements, balance sheets, and cash flow statements.

  o **Example:**

```
Sub GenerateIncomeStatement()
    Dim ws As Worksheet
    Set ws = ThisWorkbook.Sheets("Income
Statement")
```

```
ws.Range("B5").Value = "Revenue"
ws.Range("C5").Value = CalculateRevenue() '
Custom function to calculate revenue

ws.Range("B6").Value = "Cost of Goods Sold"
ws.Range("C6").Value = CalculateCOGS() '
Custom function to calculate COGS

ws.Range("B7").Value = "Gross Profit"
ws.Range("C7").Value = ws.Range("C5").Value -
ws.Range("C6").Value
End Sub
```

- **Customizing Report Layouts:** Use VBA to format and customize the layout of reports, including applying styles, creating charts, and setting print areas.

  o **Example:**

```
Sub FormatIncomeStatement()
Dim ws As Worksheet
Set ws = ThisWorkbook.Sheets("Income
Statement")

ws.Columns("B:C").AutoFit
ws.Range("B5:C7").Font.Bold = True
ws.Range("C7").Font.Color = RGB(0, 128, 0) '
Set Gross Profit to green
ws.PageSetup.Orientation = xlLandscape
ws.PageSetup.PrintArea = "B5:C20"
End Sub
```

Automating Report Distribution:

- **Emailing Reports:** Use VBA to automate the distribution of reports via email, ensuring timely delivery to stakeholders.

  o **Example:**

```
Sub EmailReport()
Dim OutlookApp As Object
```

```vba
    Dim OutlookMail As Object
    Set OutlookApp =
CreateObject("Outlook.Application")
    Set OutlookMail = OutlookApp.CreateItem(0)

    With OutlookMail
        .To = "recipient@example.com"
        .Subject = "Monthly Financial Report"
        .Body = "Please find attached the
financial report for this month."
        .Attachments.Add ThisWorkbook.FullName
        .Send
    End With
End Sub
```

- **Saving Reports to PDF:** Automate the process of saving reports as PDFs for easier sharing and archiving.

  o **Example:**

    vba

    Skopiuj kod

```vba
Sub SaveReportAsPDF()
    Dim ws As Worksheet
    Set ws = ThisWorkbook.Sheets("Income
Statement")

    ws.ExportAsFixedFormat Type:=xlTypePDF,
Filename:="C:\Reports\IncomeStatement.pdf",
Quality:=xlQualityStandard
End Sub
```

Creating custom financial reports with VBA not only improves efficiency but also ensures consistency and accuracy, enabling you to deliver high-quality reports quickly and reliably.

Case Study: Automated Budgeting Tool

Case Study: Automated Budgeting Tool

To illustrate the concepts covered in this chapter, let's walk through the development of an automated budgeting tool. This tool will automate the collection of budgeting data, perform variance analysis, and generate custom budget reports.

Step 1: Automating Data Collection

- Use VBA to pull data from various departments into a central workbook, ensuring all budget inputs are captured.

  o **Example:**

```
Sub CollectBudgetData()
    Dim ws As Worksheet
    Set ws = ThisWorkbook.Sheets("Budget")

    ' Pull data from departmental files
    ws.Range("B2").Value =
GetDepartmentData("Sales",
"C:\Budgets\Sales.xlsx")
    ws.Range("B3").Value =
GetDepartmentData("Marketing",
"C:\Budgets\Marketing.xlsx")
End Sub
```

Step 2: Automating Variance Analysis

- Automate the comparison of actual vs. budgeted figures and calculate variances.

  o **Example:**

```
Sub CalculateVariances()
    Dim ws As Worksheet
    Set ws = ThisWorkbook.Sheets("Variance
Analysis")

    ws.Range("C2").Value = ws.Range("B2").Value -
ws.Range("A2").Value ' Actual - Budget
    ws.Range("C2").NumberFormat =
"#,##0.00_);[Red](#,##0.00)"
End Sub
```

Step 3: Generating and Distributing Reports

- Create a custom budget report, format it, and distribute it to stakeholders via email.

  ○ **Example:**

```
Sub GenerateBudgetReport()
    Dim ws As Worksheet
    Set ws = ThisWorkbook.Sheets("Budget Report")

    ' Populate report
    ws.Range("B2").Value = "Department"
    ws.Range("C2").Value = "Budget"
    ws.Range("D2").Value = "Actual"
    ws.Range("E2").Value = "Variance"

    ' Format report
    ws.Columns("B:E").AutoFit
    ws.Range("B2:E2").Font.Bold = True
    ws.PageSetup.Orientation = xlPortrait

    ' Email the report
    Call EmailReport
End Sub
```

Step 4: User Interface and Automation

- Create a user-friendly interface with buttons to run the various parts of the tool, making it easy for users to execute tasks without needing to understand the underlying code.

  ○ **Example:**

```
Sub CreateUserInterface()
    Dim ws As Worksheet
    Set ws = ThisWorkbook.Sheets("Dashboard")

    ws.Buttons.Add(100, 50, 200, 30).Caption = "Collect Budget Data"
    ws.Buttons(1).OnAction = "CollectBudgetData"
```

```
    ws.Buttons.Add(100, 100, 200, 30).Caption =
"Run Variance Analysis"
    ws.Buttons(2).OnAction = "CalculateVariances"

    ws.Buttons.Add(100, 150, 200, 30).Caption =
"Generate Report"
    ws.Buttons(3).OnAction =
"GenerateBudgetReport"
End Sub
```

This automated budgeting tool illustrates how VBA can be used to streamline complex financial processes, ensuring accuracy, efficiency, and ease of use.

In this chapter, you have learned how to automate financial models using VBA, covering dynamic model building, automated financial analysis, custom report generation, and a real-world case study on an automated budgeting tool. These techniques empower you to create powerful, efficient, and scalable financial models that can save time, reduce errors, and enhance decision-making. By applying these skills, you can tackle a wide range of financial challenges with confidence, knowing that your models are robust, flexible, and ready for any scenario.

13. Data Analysis and Visualization

Data analysis and visualization are essential components of any data-driven decision-making process. Excel, combined with VBA, offers powerful tools for automating data cleaning, performing advanced analysis, and creating dynamic dashboards that help visualize complex data sets effectively. This chapter will guide you through automating data preparation, applying advanced analysis techniques, creating automated dashboards, and culminate in a case study on building an automated sales reporting system.

Automating Data Cleaning and Preparation

Before any meaningful analysis can take place, data often needs to be cleaned and prepared. This process can be time-consuming and prone to errors if done manually. VBA can automate data cleaning tasks, ensuring consistency and efficiency.

Common Data Cleaning Tasks:

1. **Removing Duplicates:**

    - Duplicate data can skew analysis results, so removing them is crucial. VBA can automate the identification and removal of duplicates.

    - **Example:**

      ```
      Sub RemoveDuplicates()
          Dim ws As Worksheet
          Set ws = ThisWorkbook.Sheets("RawData")

          ws.Range("A1:C1000").RemoveDuplicates
      Columns:=Array(1, 2), Header:=xlYes
      End Sub
      ```

2. **Handling Missing Data:**

    - Missing data can cause errors in analysis. Automate the process of identifying and handling missing values, either by filling in defaults, interpolating, or removing incomplete records.

    - **Example:**

      ```
      Sub HandleMissingData()
      ```

```
    Dim ws As Worksheet
    Set ws = ThisWorkbook.Sheets("RawData")


    ws.Range("A1:C1000").SpecialCells(xlCellTypeBlanks).Va
    lue = "N/A"
End Sub
```

3. **Standardizing Data Formats:**

   - Data from different sources may come in various formats. VBA can standardize these formats for consistent analysis.

   - **Example:**

```
Sub StandardizeDataFormats()
    Dim ws As Worksheet
    Set ws = ThisWorkbook.Sheets("RawData")

    ' Convert dates to a standard format
    ws.Range("B2:B1000").NumberFormat = "mm/dd/yyyy"
    ' Convert text to proper case
    ws.Range("C2:C1000").Value =
Application.WorksheetFunction.Proper(ws.Range("C2:C100
0").Value)
End Sub
```

4. **Data Transformation:**

   - Automate the transformation of data, such as splitting columns, concatenating data, or applying formulas across large data sets.

   - **Example:**

```
Sub TransformData()
    Dim ws As Worksheet
    Set ws = ThisWorkbook.Sheets("RawData")

    ' Combine first and last name into a single
column
    ws.Range("D2:D1000").Formula = "=A2 & "" "" & B2"
```

```
ws.Range("D2:D1000").Value =
ws.Range("D2:D1000").Value ' Convert formulas to
values
End Sub
```

By automating these data cleaning and preparation tasks, you can ensure that your data is consistent, reliable, and ready for analysis, saving valuable time and reducing the risk of errors.

Advanced Data Analysis Techniques

Advanced Data Analysis Techniques

Once your data is clean, VBA can help automate advanced data analysis techniques, allowing you to extract insights and patterns more efficiently.

Techniques for Advanced Data Analysis:

1. **Regression Analysis:**

   - Automate regression analysis to identify relationships between variables, predict trends, or forecast future values.

   - **Example:**

   ```
   Sub RunRegressionAnalysis()
       Dim ws As Worksheet
       Set ws = ThisWorkbook.Sheets("Analysis")

       ' Assuming independent variables are in columns A
   and B, and the dependent variable is in column C
       ws.Range("D1").Formula = "=LINEST(C2:C100,
   A2:B100, TRUE, TRUE)"
   End Sub
   ```

2. **Time Series Analysis:**

   - Automate the analysis of time series data to detect patterns, seasonal effects, and trends.

   - **Example:**

   ```
   Sub TimeSeriesAnalysis()
       Dim ws As Worksheet
   ```

```
Set ws = ThisWorkbook.Sheets("Analysis")

    ' Applying moving average to smooth time series
data
    ws.Range("E2:E100").Formula = "=AVERAGE(C2:C10)"
    ws.Range("E2:E100").Value =
ws.Range("E2:E100").Value ' Convert formulas to
values
End Sub
```

3. **Clustering and Segmentation:**

   - Use VBA to automate clustering techniques, such as k-means, to segment your data into meaningful groups.

   - **Example:**

```
Sub ClusterData()
    Dim ws As Worksheet
    Set ws = ThisWorkbook.Sheets("Analysis")

    ' Simple example: group data into buckets based
on value ranges
    Dim i As Integer
    For i = 2 To 100
        If ws.Cells(i, 3).Value < 50 Then
            ws.Cells(i, 4).Value = "Low"
        ElseIf ws.Cells(i, 3).Value < 100 Then
            ws.Cells(i, 4).Value = "Medium"
        Else
            ws.Cells(i, 4).Value = "High"
        End If
    Next i
End Sub
```

4. **Data Mining:**

   - Automate data mining techniques to discover patterns and relationships within large datasets.

   - **Example:**

```
Sub DataMiningAnalysis()
    Dim ws As Worksheet
    Set ws = ThisWorkbook.Sheets("Analysis")

    ' Identify frequent patterns or correlations
using correlation analysis
    ws.Range("F2:F100").Formula = "=CORREL(A2:A100,
B2:B100)"
    ws.Range("F2:F100").Value =
ws.Range("F2:F100").Value ' Convert formulas to
values
End Sub
```

By automating these advanced data analysis techniques, you can quickly uncover valuable insights and trends that inform better decision-making.

Automating the Creation of Dashboards

Automating the Creation of Dashboards

Dashboards are essential for visualizing data in a way that's easy to understand and interpret. VBA can automate the creation of dynamic dashboards, allowing you to update visualizations and metrics with a single click.

Automating Dashboard Elements:

1. **Creating Dynamic Charts:**

   - Use VBA to automatically generate and update charts based on the latest data, ensuring your dashboard always reflects the most current information.

   - **Example:**

```
Sub CreateDynamicChart()
    Dim ws As Worksheet
    Dim chartObj As ChartObject
    Set ws = ThisWorkbook.Sheets("Dashboard")

    ' Create a new chart
    Set chartObj = ws.ChartObjects.Add(Left:=100,
Width:=375, Top:=50, Height:=225)
```

```
chartObj.Chart.SetSourceData
Source:=ws.Range("A1:B10")
    chartObj.Chart.ChartType = xlColumnClustered
End Sub
```

2. **Automating KPIs and Metrics:**

   - Automate the calculation and display of key performance indicators (KPIs) on your dashboard.

   - **Example:**

```
Sub UpdateKPIs()
    Dim ws As Worksheet
    Set ws = ThisWorkbook.Sheets("Dashboard")

    ws.Range("B2").Value = "Total Sales"
    ws.Range("C2").Value =
Application.WorksheetFunction.Sum(ws.Range("SalesData"
))

    ws.Range("B3").Value = "Average Order Value"
    ws.Range("C3").Value =
Application.WorksheetFunction.Average(ws.Range("SalesD
ata"))
End Sub
```

3. **Interactive Dashboard Controls:**

   - Implement interactive controls like drop-down menus, sliders, or buttons that allow users to filter or manipulate the data displayed on the dashboard.

   - **Example:**

```
Sub CreateDropDownFilter()
    Dim ws As Worksheet
    Set ws = ThisWorkbook.Sheets("Dashboard")

    ' Create a drop-down filter for selecting regions
    ws.DropDowns.Add(Left:=100, Top:=100, Width:=100,
Height:=20).ListFillRange = "RegionsList"
```

115

```
        ws.DropDowns(1).OnAction = "FilterByRegion"
End Sub


Sub FilterByRegion()
    Dim ws As Worksheet
    Set ws = ThisWorkbook.Sheets("Dashboard")
    Dim region As String
    region = ws.DropDowns(1).Value

    ' Filter data based on selected region
    ws.Range("DataRange").AutoFilter Field:=2,
Criteria1:=region
End Sub
```

4. **Automated Refresh and Update:**

- Automate the refresh of dashboard data, ensuring that users always see the most up-to-date information.

- **Example:**

```
Sub RefreshDashboard()
    Dim ws As Worksheet
    Set ws = ThisWorkbook.Sheets("Dashboard")

    ' Refresh data connections and update
calculations
    ws.Calculate
    Call UpdateKPIs
    Call CreateDynamicChart
End Sub
```

Automating the creation and updating of dashboards ensures that your data visualizations are always current and relevant, providing decision-makers with the tools they need to make informed choices.

Case Study: Automated Sales Reporting System

To bring together the concepts covered in this chapter, let's build an automated sales reporting system. This system will clean and prepare sales data, perform advanced analysis, and generate a dynamic sales dashboard.

Step 1: Data Cleaning and Preparation

- Clean and standardize the sales data using VBA, ensuring that all data is formatted correctly and any missing or duplicate data is handled.

    - **Example:**

```
Sub PrepareSalesData()
    Dim ws As Worksheet
    Set ws = ThisWorkbook.Sheets("SalesData")

    Call RemoveDuplicates
    Call HandleMissingData
    Call StandardizeDataFormats
End Sub
```

Step 2: Advanced Sales Analysis

- Perform advanced analysis, such as calculating sales trends, forecasting future sales, and identifying key sales drivers.

    - **Example:**

```
Sub AnalyzeSalesData()
    Dim ws As Worksheet
    Set ws = ThisWorkbook.Sheets("SalesAnalysis")

    ' Calculate sales trends
    ws.Range("B2").Value =
Application.WorksheetFunction.Trend(ws.Range("Sale
sData"))

    ' Forecast future sales
    ws.Range("C2").Value =
ForecastSales(ws.Range("SalesData")) ' Custom
forecast function
End Sub
```

Step 3: Dynamic Sales Dashboard

- Create a dynamic dashboard that visualizes key sales metrics and trends, and allows users to interact with the data through filters and controls.

    o **Example:**

```
Sub GenerateSalesDashboard()
    Dim ws As Worksheet
    Set ws = ThisWorkbook.Sheets("SalesDashboard")

    ' Create KPIs
    Call UpdateKPIs

    ' Create charts
    Call CreateDynamicChart

    ' Add interactive filters
    Call CreateDropDownFilter
End Sub
```

Step 4: Automating Report Distribution

- Automate the distribution of the sales report, either by emailing it to stakeholders or saving it as a PDF for archiving.

    o **Example:**

```
Sub DistributeSalesReport()
    ' Refresh and generate the latest sales report
    Call RefreshDashboard

    ' Save the report as PDF

    ThisWorkbook.Sheets("SalesDashboard").ExportAsFixe
    dFormat Type:=xlTypePDF,
    Filename:="C:\Reports\SalesReport.pdf"

    ' Email the report to stakeholders
    Call EmailReport
End Sub
```

This automated sales reporting system demonstrates how VBA can be used to streamline the entire data analysis and reporting process, from data cleaning to advanced analysis and visualization.

In this chapter, you've learned how to automate data analysis and visualization using VBA, including automating data cleaning, performing advanced analysis, creating dynamic dashboards, and building a comprehensive automated sales reporting system. These skills will enable you to handle large datasets more efficiently, extract deeper insights from your data, and present those insights in a clear and compelling way. Whether you're creating a one-off report or developing a system for ongoing analysis, the techniques covered in this chapter will help you deliver high-quality results quickly and consistently.

14. Managing Projects with Excel VBA

Project management involves planning, scheduling, tracking progress, and optimizing resources to achieve project goals efficiently. Excel is a powerful tool for managing projects, and by leveraging VBA, you can automate many of the repetitive and time-consuming tasks involved in project management. In this chapter, you will learn how to automate project plans and schedules, track project progress, optimize resource allocation, and create automated Gantt charts to visualize project timelines. A case study on automated Gantt chart creation will demonstrate the practical application of these techniques.

Automating Project Plans and Schedules

Creating and managing project plans and schedules in Excel can be a complex task, especially for large projects with many moving parts. VBA can help automate the creation of project plans, ensuring that schedules are accurate and updated regularly.

Automating Task Lists:

- **Generating Task Lists:** Use VBA to automatically generate task lists based on project templates or input data. This ensures that all necessary tasks are included and organized logically.

  o **Example:**

```
Sub GenerateTaskList()
    Dim ws As Worksheet
    Set ws = ThisWorkbook.Sheets("TaskList")

    ws.Range("A1").Value = "Task ID"
    ws.Range("B1").Value = "Task Name"
    ws.Range("C1").Value = "Start Date"
    ws.Range("D1").Value = "End Date"
    ws.Range("E1").Value = "Assigned To"

    ' Example tasks
    ws.Range("A2:E6").Value = Array( _
        Array(1, "Define Project Scope", _
    "01/01/2024", "01/05/2024", "John"), _
```

```
        Array(2, "Gather Requirements",
"01/06/2024", "01/15/2024", "Jane"), _
        Array(3, "Design Solution", "01/16/2024",
"01/25/2024", "John"), _
        Array(4, "Develop Solution", "01/26/2024",
"02/10/2024", "Mike"), _
        Array(5, "Test Solution", "02/11/2024",
"02/20/2024", "Jane"))
End Sub
```

- **Scheduling Tasks:** Automate the scheduling of tasks by calculating start and end dates based on task dependencies and project milestones.

  ○ **Example:**

```
Sub ScheduleTasks()
    Dim ws As Worksheet
    Set ws = ThisWorkbook.Sheets("TaskList")

    Dim lastRow As Long
    lastRow = ws.Cells(ws.Rows.Count,
"A").End(xlUp).Row

    Dim i As Long
    For i = 2 To lastRow
        If ws.Cells(i, 3).Value = "" Then
            ' Start Date based on end date of
previous task
            ws.Cells(i, 3).Value = ws.Cells(i - 1,
4).Value + 1
            ' End Date based on task duration
(example: 5 days)
            ws.Cells(i, 4).Value = ws.Cells(i,
3).Value + 5
        End If
    Next i
End Sub
```

Automating Milestone Tracking:

- **Setting Milestones:** Use VBA to automatically identify and track project milestones based on the task list. Milestones can be highlighted or separated for easy tracking.

  o **Example:**

```
Sub SetMilestones()
    Dim ws As Worksheet
    Set ws = ThisWorkbook.Sheets("TaskList")

    Dim i As Long
    For i = 2 To ws.Cells(ws.Rows.Count,
"A").End(xlUp).Row
        If ws.Cells(i, 2).Value Like "*Milestone*"
Then
            ws.Rows(i).Interior.Color = RGB(255,
255, 0) ' Highlight milestone row in yellow
        End If
    Next i
End Sub
```

Dynamic Project Calendars:

- **Creating a Dynamic Calendar:** Automate the creation of a project calendar that dynamically updates as task dates change, ensuring that your schedule is always accurate.

  o **Example:**

```
Sub CreateProjectCalendar()
    Dim ws As Worksheet
    Set ws =
ThisWorkbook.Sheets("ProjectCalendar")

    Dim taskWs As Worksheet
    Set taskWs = ThisWorkbook.Sheets("TaskList")

    Dim i As Long, j As Long
    Dim startDate As Date, endDate As Date
```

```
ws.Cells.Clear
ws.Range("A1").Value = "Date"
ws.Range("B1").Value = "Task"

For i = 2 To taskWs.Cells(taskWs.Rows.Count,
"A").End(xlUp).Row
    startDate = taskWs.Cells(i, 3).Value
    endDate = taskWs.Cells(i, 4).Value

    For j = startDate To endDate
        ws.Cells(j - startDate + 2, 1).Value =
j
        ws.Cells(j - startDate + 2, 2).Value =
taskWs.Cells(i, 2).Value
        Next j
    Next i
End Sub
```

By automating the creation and management of project plans and schedules, you can ensure that your project timelines are always up-to-date and aligned with the project's goals and constraints.

Tracking Project Progress with VBA

Tracking project progress is critical for ensuring that tasks are completed on time and within budget. VBA can automate the process of updating and visualizing project progress, making it easier to identify potential issues and take corrective action.

Automating Progress Tracking:

- **Updating Task Status:** Use VBA to automate the updating of task status based on progress reports from team members.

  - **Example:**

    ```
    Sub UpdateTaskStatus()
    Dim ws As Worksheet
    Set ws = ThisWorkbook.Sheets("TaskList")
    ```

```
Dim lastRow As Long
lastRow = ws.Cells(ws.Rows.Count,
"A").End(xlUp).Row

Dim i As Long
For i = 2 To lastRow
    If Date >= ws.Cells(i, 4).Value Then
        ws.Cells(i, 6).Value = "Complete"
    ElseIf Date >= ws.Cells(i, 3).Value Then
        ws.Cells(i, 6).Value = "In Progress"
    Else
        ws.Cells(i, 6).Value = "Not Started"
    End If
Next i
End Sub
```

- **Visualizing Progress with Conditional Formatting:** Automate the application of conditional formatting to visualize project progress, such as color-coding tasks based on their status.

  o **Example:**

```
Sub ApplyConditionalFormatting()
    Dim ws As Worksheet
    Set ws = ThisWorkbook.Sheets("TaskList")

    ws.Columns("F:F").ClearFormats

    With ws.Range("F2:F100")
        .FormatConditions.Add Type:=xlCellValue,
Operator:=xlEqual, Formula1:="=""Complete"""
        .FormatConditions(1).Interior.Color =
RGB(0, 255, 0) ' Green for Complete

        .FormatConditions.Add Type:=xlCellValue,
Operator:=xlEqual, Formula1:="=""In Progress"""
        .FormatConditions(2).Interior.Color =
RGB(255, 255, 0) ' Yellow for In Progress
```

```
        .FormatConditions.Add Type:=xlCellValue,
    Operator:=xlEqual, Formula1:="=""Not Started"""
        .FormatConditions(3).Interior.Color =
    RGB(255, 0, 0) ' Red for Not Started
        End With
    End Sub
```

Generating Progress Reports:

- **Automating Status Reports:** Use VBA to generate regular status reports that summarize project progress, highlight delays, and provide an overview of completed and pending tasks.

    o **Example:**

```
Sub GenerateStatusReport()
    Dim ws As Worksheet
    Set ws = ThisWorkbook.Sheets("StatusReport")

    ws.Cells.Clear
    ws.Range("A1").Value = "Task"
    ws.Range("B1").Value = "Status"
    ws.Range("C1").Value = "Assigned To"
    ws.Range("D1").Value = "Due Date"

    Dim taskWs As Worksheet
    Set taskWs = ThisWorkbook.Sheets("TaskList")

    Dim i As Long
    For i = 2 To taskWs.Cells(taskWs.Rows.Count,
"A").End(xlUp).Row
        ws.Cells(i, 1).Value = taskWs.Cells(i,
2).Value
        ws.Cells(i, 2).Value = taskWs.Cells(i,
6).Value
        ws.Cells(i, 3).Value = taskWs.Cells(i,
5).Value
```

```
                    ws.Cells(i, 4).Value = taskWs.Cells(i,
        4).Value
            Next i


            ws.Columns.AutoFit
        End Sub
```

Automated Alerts and Notifications:

- **Setting Up Alerts for Delayed Tasks:** Use VBA to automatically send alerts or notifications when tasks are delayed or deadlines are approaching.

  o **Example:**

```
        Sub SendAlertsForDelayedTasks()
            Dim ws As Worksheet
            Set ws = ThisWorkbook.Sheets("TaskList")

            Dim i As Long
            For i = 2 To ws.Cells(ws.Rows.Count,
        "A").End(xlUp).Row
                    If Date > ws.Cells(i, 4).Value And
        ws.Cells(i, 6).Value <> "Complete" Then
                        MsgBox "Task " & ws.Cells(i, 2).Value
        & " is delayed!", vbExclamation
                    End If
                Next i
            End Sub
```

Automating the tracking of project progress ensures that project managers can quickly identify and address issues, keeping the project on track and stakeholders informed.

Resource Allocation and Optimization

Efficient resource allocation is key to successful project management. VBA can help optimize resource allocation by automating the assignment of tasks, balancing workloads, and identifying resource constraints.

Automating Resource Allocation:

- **Assigning Tasks Based on Availability:** Use VBA to automatically assign tasks to team members based on their availability and workload.

    o **Example:**

```
Sub AllocateResources()
    Dim ws As Worksheet
    Set ws = ThisWorkbook.Sheets("TaskList")

    Dim i As Long
    For i = 2 To ws.Cells(ws.Rows.Count,
"A").End(xlUp).Row
        If ws.Cells(i, 5).Value = "" Then ' If
task is not assigned
            ws.Cells(i, 5).Value =
AssignToAvailableResource()
        End If
    Next i
End Sub


Function AssignToAvailableResource() As String
    ' Example logic for assigning task to the
least busy resource
    ' This could be expanded with more complex
logic based on workload
    AssignToAvailableResource = "John" '
Placeholder for logic
End Function
```

Optimizing Resource Utilization:

- **Balancing Workloads:** Automate the balancing of workloads to ensure that no single resource is overburdened and that tasks are evenly distributed.

    o **Example:**

```
Sub BalanceWorkloads()
    Dim ws As Worksheet
```

```vba
Set ws = ThisWorkbook.Sheets("TaskList")

Dim i As Long, workload As Integer
Dim resource As String

For i = 2 To ws.Cells(ws.Rows.Count,
"A").End(xlUp).Row
        resource = ws.Cells(i, 5).Value
        workload = GetResourceWorkload(resource)

        If workload > 40 Then ' Example threshold
for workload
            MsgBox "Resource " & resource & " is
overburdened. Reassigning tasks.", vbExclamation
                ws.Cells(i, 5).Value =
AssignToAvailableResource()
        End If
    Next i
End Sub

Function GetResourceWorkload(resource As String)
As Integer
    ' Placeholder for logic to calculate the
workload of a given resource
    GetResourceWorkload = 40 ' Example workload
End Function
```

Resource Constraint Analysis:

- **Identifying Resource Bottlenecks:** Use VBA to identify resource bottlenecks that could delay the project, allowing for proactive reallocation or rescheduling.

    o **Example:**

    ```vba
    Sub IdentifyResourceBottlenecks()
        Dim ws As Worksheet
        Set ws = ThisWorkbook.Sheets("TaskList")
    ```

```vba
Dim i As Long
For i = 2 To ws.Cells(ws.Rows.Count,
"A").End(xlUp).Row
    If ws.Cells(i, 6).Value = "In Progress"
And ResourceOverloaded(ws.Cells(i, 5).Value) Then
        MsgBox "Resource " & ws.Cells(i,
5).Value & " is overloaded. Task " & ws.Cells(i,
2).Value & " may be delayed.", vbExclamation
    End If
Next i
End Sub


Function ResourceOverloaded(resource As String) As
Boolean
    ' Placeholder for logic to check if a resource
is overloaded
    ResourceOverloaded = False ' Example return
value
End Function
```

By automating resource allocation and optimization, you can ensure that your project is staffed appropriately and that resources are used efficiently, reducing the likelihood of delays and cost overruns.

Case Study: Automated Gantt Chart Creation

A Gantt chart is a fundamental tool in project management for visualizing the timeline of a project. Creating Gantt charts manually can be time-consuming, especially for large projects. In this case study, we'll automate the creation of a Gantt chart using VBA.

Step 1: Preparing the Data

- **Ensure Task Data is Structured:** The task list should include columns for task name, start date, end date, duration, and assigned resource.

    o **Example:**

```vba
Sub PrepareGanttData()
    Dim ws As Worksheet
    Set ws = ThisWorkbook.Sheets("TaskList")
```

```
ws.Range("G1").Value = "Duration"
ws.Range("G2:G100").Formula = "=D2-C2+1" '
```
Calculate task duration
```
End Sub
```

Step 2: Creating the Gantt Chart

- **Automate Chart Creation:** Use VBA to automatically create a Gantt chart that visualizes the project timeline.

  o **Example:**

```
Sub CreateGanttChart()
    Dim ws As Worksheet
    Set ws = ThisWorkbook.Sheets("GanttChart")

    Dim taskWs As Worksheet
    Set taskWs = ThisWorkbook.Sheets("TaskList")

    Dim i As Long
    Dim startDate As Date, endDate As Date

    ' Clear previous chart data
    ws.Cells.Clear

    ' Set up the Gantt chart headers
    ws.Range("A1").Value = "Task"
    ws.Range("B1").Value = "Start Date"
    ws.Range("C1").Value = "End Date"
    ws.Range("D1").Value = "Gantt Chart"

    ' Populate the Gantt chart data
    For i = 2 To taskWs.Cells(taskWs.Rows.Count,
"A").End(xlUp).Row
        startDate = taskWs.Cells(i, 3).Value
        endDate = taskWs.Cells(i, 4).Value
```

```
            ws.Cells(i, 1).Value = taskWs.Cells(i,
2).Value
            ws.Cells(i, 2).Value = startDate
            ws.Cells(i, 3).Value = endDate

        ' Create Gantt bars
            ws.Cells(i, 4).Resize(1, endDate -
startDate + 1).Interior.Color = RGB(0, 0, 255)
        Next i

        ws.Columns.AutoFit
    End Sub
```

Step 3: Enhancing the Gantt Chart

- **Add Milestones and Dependencies:** Use VBA to highlight milestones and show task dependencies on the Gantt chart.

  o **Example:**

```
Sub EnhanceGanttChart()
    Dim ws As Worksheet
    Set ws = ThisWorkbook.Sheets("GanttChart")

    ' Highlight milestones
    Dim i As Long
    For i = 2 To ws.Cells(ws.Rows.Count,
"A").End(xlUp).Row
        If ws.Cells(i, 1).Value Like "*Milestone*"
Then
            ws.Cells(i, 4).Interior.Color =
RGB(255, 255, 0) ' Highlight milestone in yellow
        End If
    Next i

    ' Show dependencies (e.g., with arrows or
colored lines)
    ' Placeholder for logic to display
dependencies
```

```
End Sub
```

Step 4: Automating Updates

- **Automatically Update the Gantt Chart:** Ensure that the Gantt chart updates automatically when task dates change, keeping the timeline accurate and up-to-date.

  - **Example:**

    ```
    Sub UpdateGanttChart()
        Call PrepareGanttData
        Call CreateGanttChart
        Call EnhanceGanttChart
    End Sub
    ```

This automated Gantt chart creation process demonstrates how VBA can streamline the visualization of project timelines, making it easier to manage and communicate project schedules.

In this chapter, you've learned how to manage projects with Excel VBA, including automating project plans and schedules, tracking progress, optimizing resource allocation, and creating automated Gantt charts. These techniques will help you manage projects more efficiently, ensuring that tasks are completed on time, resources are used effectively, and project timelines are communicated clearly. By applying these skills, you can enhance your project management capabilities, delivering projects that meet their goals and deadlines with greater accuracy and efficiency.

15. Automating Repetitive Tasks in Excel

One of the most powerful features of VBA in Excel is its ability to automate repetitive tasks, saving time and reducing the potential for human error. In this chapter, we will explore how to automate routine reporting tasks, process bulk data efficiently, create reusable macro libraries, and implement these techniques in a case study focused on automating HR reports and payroll processing.

Automating Routine Reporting Tasks

Routine reporting can be time-consuming and prone to errors, especially when performed manually on a regular basis. By automating these tasks with VBA, you can ensure that reports are generated accurately and consistently, freeing up time for more strategic activities.

Automating Report Generation:

- **Standard Reports:** Use VBA to automate the generation of standard reports, such as monthly sales summaries, inventory reports, or financial statements.

    - **Example:**

```
Sub GenerateMonthlySalesReport()
    Dim ws As Worksheet
    Set ws = ThisWorkbook.Sheets("SalesReport")

    ' Clear previous report data
    ws.Cells.Clear

    ' Generate new report
    ws.Range("A1").Value = "Product"
    ws.Range("B1").Value = "Total Sales"

    ws.Range("A2").Value = "Product A"
    ws.Range("B2").Value =
Application.WorksheetFunction.SumIf(Range("SalesDa
ta!A:A"), "Product A", Range("SalesData!B:B"))
```

```
        ws.Range("A3").Value = "Product B"
        ws.Range("B3").Value =
Application.WorksheetFunction.SumIf(Range("SalesDa
ta!A:A"), "Product B", Range("SalesData!B:B"))

        ' Format report
        ws.Columns.AutoFit
End Sub
```

- **Automating Report Distribution:** Automatically email reports to stakeholders once they are generated, ensuring timely delivery.

  o **Example:**

```
Sub EmailSalesReport()
        Dim OutlookApp As Object
        Dim MailItem As Object
        Dim ws As Worksheet
        Set ws = ThisWorkbook.Sheets("SalesReport")

        ' Generate the report
        Call GenerateMonthlySalesReport

        ' Set up Outlook
        Set OutlookApp =
CreateObject("Outlook.Application")
        Set MailItem = OutlookApp.CreateItem(0)

        ' Compose email
        With MailItem
            .To = "recipient@example.com"
            .Subject = "Monthly Sales Report"
            .Body = "Please find the attached sales
report for this month."
            .Attachments.Add ws.Parent.FullName
            .Send
        End With
End Sub
```

Scheduled Report Execution:

- **Using Windows Task Scheduler:** You can set up your VBA macro to run at specific intervals using the Windows Task Scheduler, ensuring that reports are generated and distributed on a regular basis without manual intervention.

    o **Example:**

        ▪ Save your macro-enabled workbook (.**xlsm**) and create a script to open it in Excel.

        ▪ Schedule this script to run at your desired intervals using Task Scheduler.

Automating Report Customization:

- **Customizable Reports:** Allow users to customize the parameters of reports, such as date ranges or regions, using input forms or parameter fields.

    o **Example:**

```
Sub GenerateCustomSalesReport()
    Dim ws As Worksheet
    Set ws = ThisWorkbook.Sheets("SalesReport")

    Dim startDate As Date
    Dim endDate As Date

    ' Get user input for report parameters
    startDate = InputBox("Enter the start date
(MM/DD/YYYY):", "Start Date")
    endDate = InputBox("Enter the end date
(MM/DD/YYYY):", "End Date")

    ' Generate report based on user input
    ws.Cells.Clear
    ws.Range("A1").Value = "Product"
    ws.Range("B1").Value = "Total Sales"
    ws.Range("A2").Value = "Product A"
```

```
        ws.Range("B2").Value =
    Application.WorksheetFunction.SumIfs( _
            Range("SalesData!B:B"),
    Range("SalesData!A:A"), "Product A",
    Range("SalesData!C:C"), ">=" & startDate,
    Range("SalesData!C:C"), "<=" & endDate)


        ' Format report
        ws.Columns.AutoFit
    End Sub
```

Automating routine reporting tasks ensures that essential reports are produced efficiently, with minimal manual effort, and are delivered consistently to the right people.

Bulk Data Processing with VBA

Processing large amounts of data manually can be labor-intensive and error-prone. VBA can automate the processing of bulk data, making it faster and more reliable.

Batch Processing of Data:

- **Looping Through Large Data Sets:** Use VBA to loop through large datasets and perform operations such as data transformation, aggregation, or cleansing.

    o **Example:**

```
    Sub ProcessBulkData()
        Dim ws As Worksheet
        Set ws = ThisWorkbook.Sheets("Data")

        Dim lastRow As Long
        lastRow = ws.Cells(ws.Rows.Count,
    "A").End(xlUp).Row

        Dim i As Long
        For i = 2 To lastRow
            ' Example: Standardize text to proper case
```

```
        ws.Cells(i, 2).Value =
Application.WorksheetFunction.Proper(ws.Cells(i,
2).Value)
        Next i
End Sub
```

Data Consolidation:

- **Consolidating Data from Multiple Sources:** Automate the consolidation of data from multiple workbooks or sheets into a single report or dataset.

  - **Example:**

```
Sub ConsolidateData()
    Dim ws As Worksheet
    Set ws =
ThisWorkbook.Sheets("ConsolidatedData")

    Dim sourceWb As Workbook
    Dim sourceWs As Worksheet
    Dim i As Long

    ' List of workbooks to consolidate
    Dim filePaths As Variant
    filePaths = Array("C:\Data\Source1.xlsx",
"C:\Data\Source2.xlsx")

    ' Clear previous data
    ws.Cells.Clear

    ' Loop through each workbook and consolidate
data
    For i = LBound(filePaths) To UBound(filePaths)
        Set sourceWb =
Workbooks.Open(filePaths(i))
        Set sourceWs = sourceWb.Sheets(1) '
Assuming data is in the first sheet
```

```
        sourceWs.Range("A1:B100").Copy
    Destination:=ws.Cells(ws.Rows.Count,
    "A").End(xlUp).Offset(1, 0)
        sourceWb.Close SaveChanges:=False
    Next i
End Sub
```

Data Validation and Cleansing:

- **Automating Data Validation:** Use VBA to automate the validation of data according to specific business rules, ensuring data integrity before processing.

  o **Example:**

```
Sub ValidateData()
    Dim ws As Worksheet
    Set ws = ThisWorkbook.Sheets("Data")

    Dim lastRow As Long
    lastRow = ws.Cells(ws.Rows.Count,
    "A").End(xlUp).Row

    Dim i As Long
    For i = 2 To lastRow
        ' Example: Validate email format
        If Not ws.Cells(i, 3).Value Like "*@*.*"
    Then
            ws.Cells(i, 4).Value = "Invalid Email"
        Else
            ws.Cells(i, 4).Value = "Valid Email"
        End If
    Next i
End Sub
```

By automating bulk data processing, you can handle large volumes of data more efficiently, ensuring that tasks like data consolidation, transformation, and validation are performed quickly and accurately.

Creating Reusable Macro Libraries

Reusable macro libraries allow you to store and manage common VBA functions and procedures that can be used across multiple projects, saving time and promoting consistency.

Building a Macro Library:

- **Organizing Common Functions:** Create a dedicated workbook or module where you store commonly used functions and procedures.

    o **Example:**

    ```
    ' File: MacroLibrary.bas
    ' Description: A collection of reusable VBA
    functions

    ' Function to calculate the average of a range
    Function CalculateAverage(rng As Range) As Double
        CalculateAverage =
    Application.WorksheetFunction.Average(rng)
    End Function

    ' Function to convert a string to title case
    Function ConvertToTitleCase(text As String) As
    String
        ConvertToTitleCase =
    Application.WorksheetFunction.Proper(text)
    End Function
    ```

Accessing the Macro Library:

- **Referencing the Library:** You can reference your macro library in other workbooks by importing the module or by creating an Excel add-in that houses your library.

    o **Example:**

    ```
    ' In another workbook
    Sub UseMacroLibrary()
        Dim avg As Double
    ```

```
    avg =
CalculateAverage(ThisWorkbook.Sheets("Data").Range
("A1:A10"))

    MsgBox "The average is " & avg
End Sub
```

Maintaining the Library:

- **Version Control:** Keep track of changes to your macro library by implementing version control, ensuring that you can easily update and maintain your functions.

  o **Example:**

```
' Add version number to your macro library
Public Const LibraryVersion As String = "1.0.0"
```

- **Documentation:** Document each function and procedure in your library to ensure that others (or you, in the future) can easily understand how to use them.

  o **Example:**

```
' Function: CalculateAverage
' Description: Calculates the average of a given
range of cells.
' Parameters: rng (Range) - The range of cells to
average.
' Returns: Double - The calculated average.

Function CalculateAverage(rng As Range) As Double
    CalculateAverage =
Application.WorksheetFunction.Average(rng)
End Function
```

Creating reusable macro libraries ensures that your VBA code is modular, maintainable, and easy to reuse across different projects, leading to more efficient development and consistent results.

Case Study: Automating HR Reports and Payroll Processing

To bring together the concepts discussed in this chapter, let's walk through the development of an automated system for generating HR reports and processing payroll.

Step 1: Automating HR Reports

- **Employee Data Processing:** Automate the process of consolidating employee data from multiple sources into a single report, ensuring data accuracy and completeness.

    o **Example:**

```
Sub GenerateHRReport()
    Dim ws As Worksheet
    Set ws = ThisWorkbook.Sheets("HRReport")

    ' Consolidate employee data
    Call ConsolidateData

    ' Process and format the report
    ws.Range("A1").Value = "Employee ID"
    ws.Range("B1").Value = "Name"
    ws.Range("C1").Value = "Department"
    ws.Range("D1").Value = "Position"
    ws.Range("E1").Value = "Salary"

    ' Example: Calculate total salaries
    ws.Range("E2:E100").Formula =
"=SUMIF(EmployeeData!C:C, B2, EmployeeData!D:D)"
    ws.Columns.AutoFit
End Sub
```

Step 2: Automating Payroll Processing

- **Calculating Payroll:** Automate the calculation of payroll based on hours worked, overtime, bonuses, and deductions, ensuring accurate and timely payroll processing.

    o **Example:**

```
Sub ProcessPayroll()
    Dim ws As Worksheet
    Set ws = ThisWorkbook.Sheets("Payroll")

    Dim lastRow As Long
    lastRow = ws.Cells(ws.Rows.Count,
"A").End(xlUp).Row

    Dim i As Long
    For i = 2 To lastRow
        ' Calculate gross pay
        ws.Cells(i, 5).Value = ws.Cells(i,
3).Value * ws.Cells(i, 4).Value ' Hours * Rate

        ' Calculate deductions (example: 20% tax)
        ws.Cells(i, 6).Value = ws.Cells(i,
5).Value * 0.2

        ' Calculate net pay
        ws.Cells(i, 7).Value = ws.Cells(i,
5).Value - ws.Cells(i, 6).Value
    Next i
End Sub
```

Step 3: Automating Report Distribution

- **Distributing Payroll Reports:** Automate the distribution of payroll reports to individual employees via email, ensuring confidentiality and timely delivery.

  - **Example:**

```
Sub EmailPayrollReports()
    Dim ws As Worksheet
    Set ws = ThisWorkbook.Sheets("Payroll")

    Dim OutlookApp As Object
    Dim MailItem As Object
    Dim i As Long
```

```vba
' Set up Outlook
Set OutlookApp =
CreateObject("Outlook.Application")

' Loop through each employee and send payroll
report
For i = 2 To ws.Cells(ws.Rows.Count,
"A").End(xlUp).Row
    Set MailItem = OutlookApp.CreateItem(0)

    With MailItem
        .To = ws.Cells(i, 2).Value ' Employee
email
        .Subject = "Your Payroll Report"
        .Body = "Dear " & ws.Cells(i, 3).Value
& ", please find your payroll report attached."
        .Attachments.Add ws.Parent.FullName
        .Send
    End With
Next i
End Sub
```

Step 4: Reusing and Maintaining the System

- **Leveraging Macro Libraries:** Integrate reusable functions from your macro library to handle common tasks, such as data validation or formatting, ensuring consistency and maintainability.

  o **Example:**

```vba
Sub GeneratePayrollReport()
    Dim ws As Worksheet
    Set ws = ThisWorkbook.Sheets("Payroll")

    ' Reuse functions from the macro library
    ws.Range("A2:A100").Value =
ConvertToTitleCase(ws.Range("A2:A100").Value)
    Call ProcessPayroll
```

```
        Call EmailPayrollReports
    End Sub
```

This automated HR and payroll processing system demonstrates how VBA can streamline complex workflows, ensuring that reports and payroll are processed accurately, efficiently, and consistently.

In this chapter, you've learned how to automate repetitive tasks in Excel, including automating routine reporting, processing bulk data, creating reusable macro libraries, and applying these techniques in a real-world case study. By leveraging VBA to automate these tasks, you can significantly reduce manual effort, increase accuracy, and improve efficiency across a wide range of Excel-based activities. Whether you're generating reports, processing data, or managing payroll, the skills covered in this chapter will help you create powerful, automated solutions that save time and deliver consistent results.

Part V: Appendices

In this final section of the book, we provide a set of appendices designed to support your journey in mastering Excel VBA. These appendices include a comprehensive list of common VBA functions and their uses, a reference guide for quick lookup, troubleshooting tips, frequently asked questions, recommended resources for further learning, and a collection of sample projects to practice your skills. Whether you're a beginner or an experienced VBA developer, these resources will serve as a valuable reference and guide as you continue to explore and apply VBA in your work.

Appendix A: Common VBA Functions and Their Uses

Understanding the most commonly used VBA functions is crucial for efficient coding. This appendix provides a list of essential VBA functions along with descriptions and examples of how to use them.

1. String Functions:

- **Left and Right**: Extracts a specified number of characters from the beginning or end of a string.

    o **Example: Left("Hello", 2)** returns **"He"**.

- **Mid**: Extracts characters from a string, starting at any position.

    o **Example: Mid("Hello", 2, 2)** returns "el".

- **Len**: Returns the length of a string.

    o **Example: Len("Hello")** returns **5**.

2. Date and Time Functions:

- **Date**: Returns the current date.

    o **Example: Date** might return **08/30/2024**.

- **Time**: Returns the current time.

    o **Example: Time** might return **14:30:00**.

- **DateAdd**: Adds a specified interval to a date.

o **Example: DateAdd("d", 10, Date)** adds 10 days to the current date.

3. Math Functions:

- **Abs**: Returns the absolute value of a number.

    o **Example: Abs(-10)** returns **10.**

- **Round**: Rounds a number to a specified number of decimal places.

    o **Example: Round(3.14159, 2)** returns **3.14.**

- **Sqr**: Returns the square root of a number.

    o **Example: Sqr(16)** returns **4.**

4. Logical Functions:

- **If**: Executes a block of code if a condition is true.

    o **Example: If x > 10 Then MsgBox "x is greater than 10".**

- **IIf**: Returns one of two values depending on the evaluation of an expression.

    o **Example: IIf(x > 10, "Greater", "Less or Equal").**

- **Select Case**: Executes one of several groups of statements, depending on the value of an expression.

    o **Example:**

```
Select Case x
    Case 1
        MsgBox "One"
    Case 2
        MsgBox "Two"
    Case Else
        MsgBox "Other"
End Select
```

5. Array Functions:

- **LBound and UBound**: Returns the lower and upper bounds of an array.

- o **Example:**

```
Dim arr(1 To 10) As Integer
LBound(arr) ' Returns 1
UBound(arr) ' Returns 10
```

- **Split**: Splits a string into an array based on a delimiter.

  - o **Example: Split("a,b,c", ",")** returns an array **("a", "b", "c").**

- **Join**: Joins an array of strings into a single string.

  - o **Example: Join(Array("a", "b", "c"), ",")** returns **"a,b,c".**

6. File Handling Functions:

- **Dir**: Returns the name of a file or directory that matches a pattern.

  - o **Example: Dir("C:*.txt")** returns the first **.txt** file in the directory.

- **FileCopy**: Copies a file from one location to another.

  - o **Example: FileCopy "C:\file1.txt", "C:\backup\file1.txt".**

- **Kill**: Deletes a file.

  - o **Example: Kill "C:\file1.txt".**

This appendix serves as a quick reference for these and other essential functions, enabling you to quickly find and apply the functions you need in your VBA projects.

Appendix B: VBA Reference Guide

The VBA Reference Guide provides detailed descriptions of key VBA concepts, objects, properties, and methods. It is intended as a quick lookup tool for developers working on complex projects.

1. The VBA Object Model:

- **Application Object**: Represents the entire Excel application.

  - o **Example: Application.Calculation = xlCalculationManual** turns off automatic calculations.

- **Workbook Object**: Represents an Excel workbook.

- o **Example:** **Workbooks("Book1.xlsx").Save** saves the workbook.

- **Worksheet Object**: Represents a worksheet within a workbook.

  - o **Example:** **Worksheets("Sheet1").Range("A1").Value** = **"Hello"** sets the value of cell A1.

2. Common Properties and Methods:

- **Range Properties**:

  - o **Value**: Gets or sets the value of a cell.

    - ▪ **Example: Range("A1").Value = 100**.

  - o **Formula**: Gets or sets the formula in a cell.

    - ▪ **Example:** **Range("A1").Formula** = **"=SUM(B1:B10)"**.

  - o **Interior.Color**: Sets the background color of a cell.

    - ▪ **Example: Range("A1").Interior.Color = RGB(255, 0, 0)** sets the cell color to red.

- **Worksheet Methods**:

  - o **Copy**: Copies a worksheet to another location.

    - ▪ **Example:** **Worksheets("Sheet1").Copy After:=Worksheets("Sheet2")**.

  - o **Delete**: Deletes a worksheet.

    - ▪ **Example: Worksheets("Sheet1").Delete**.

- **Workbook Methods**:

  - o **Close**: Closes a workbook.

    - ▪ **Example:** **Workbooks("Book1.xlsx").Close SaveChanges:=True**.

  - o **SaveAs**: Saves a workbook with a new name.

    - ▪ **Example:** **Workbooks("Book1.xlsx").SaveAs "C:\NewBook.xlsx"**.

3. Events in VBA:

- **Workbook Events:**

  - **Workbook_Open**: Runs when a workbook is opened.

    - **Example: Private Sub Workbook_Open()** initializes settings when the workbook opens.

- **Worksheet Events:**

  - **Worksheet_Change**: Runs when a cell value changes.

    - **Example: Private Sub Worksheet_Change(ByVal Target As Range)** handles changes in the worksheet.

- **Application Events:**

  - **Application_OnTime**: Schedules a procedure to run at a specified time.

    - **Example: Application.OnTime Now + TimeValue("00:01:00"), "MyMacro"** runs MyMacro in one minute.

This reference guide provides quick access to detailed information about VBA objects, properties, methods, and events, helping you to write more efficient and powerful VBA code.

Appendix C: Troubleshooting and FAQs

This appendix addresses common issues and questions that arise when working with VBA. Whether you're facing an error, debugging code, or trying to understand a tricky concept, this section provides practical solutions.

1. Common VBA Errors and Solutions:

- **Compile Error: Syntax Error:**

  - **Cause**: Mistyped code, such as missing a parenthesis or misspelling a keyword.

  - **Solution**: Check your syntax and ensure all elements are properly formatted.

- **Runtime Error: Object Variable Not Set**:

  - **Cause**: A variable that should reference an object hasn't been initialized.

  - **Solution**: Ensure that your object variables are correctly set with **Set,** such as **Set ws = ThisWorkbook.Sheets("Sheet1").**

- **Runtime Error: Subscript Out of Range**:

  - **Cause**: Trying to access a worksheet or array element that doesn't exist.

  - **Solution**: Verify that the worksheet or array index is valid and exists.

2. Debugging Tips:

- **Using Breakpoints**: Set breakpoints in your code to pause execution and examine the current state.

  - **Example**: Click in the margin next to a line of code in the VBA editor to set a breakpoint.

- **Watch Windows**: Use the Watch Window to monitor the values of variables or expressions as your code runs.

  - **Example**: Right-click a variable and select "Add Watch" to track its value.

- **Immediate Window**: Execute lines of code directly and check the results in real-time.

  - **Example**: Type **? Range("A1").Value** in the Immediate Window to see the value of cell A1.

3. Frequently Asked Questions:

- **How do I create a macro that runs automatically when a workbook opens?**

  - **Answer**: Place your code in the **Workbook_Open** event in the ThisWorkbook module.

- **How can I protect my VBA code from being viewed or edited by others?**

- o **Answer**: Use the "VBAProject Properties" dialog to lock your project with a password.

- **Can I run a macro at a specific time every day?**

  - o **Answer**: Yes, use the **Application.OnTime** method to schedule a macro to run at a specific time.

This appendix serves as a quick troubleshooting guide, helping you to solve common problems and understand how to work through issues as they arise in your VBA projects.

Appendix D: Useful Resources and Further Reading

Continuous learning is key to mastering VBA. This appendix provides a list of resources, books, websites, and forums where you can deepen your knowledge and find solutions to advanced problems.

1. Books:

- **"Excel 2019 Power Programming with VBA" by Michael Alexander and Dick Kusleika**: A comprehensive guide for advanced VBA programming.

- **"VBA for Modelers: Developing Decision Support Systems with Microsoft Office Excel" by S. Christian Albright**: Focuses on using VBA for business modeling.

2. Online Resources:

- **Microsoft's Official VBA Documentation**: Provides detailed documentation and examples directly from Microsoft.

  - o **Link**: Microsoft VBA Documentation

- **Stack Overflow**: A community-driven site where you can ask questions and find answers to VBA-related issues.

  - o **Link**: Stack Overflow VBA

3. Forums and Communities:

- **MrExcel Forum**: A popular forum for Excel users, with a dedicated section for VBA questions.

  - o **Link**: MrExcel Forum

- **Reddit VBA**: A subreddit where users discuss VBA tips, tricks, and challenges.

    o **Link**: Reddit VBA

4. Video Tutorials:

- **YouTube Channels**:

    o **Excel Campus**: Offers tutorials on VBA and advanced Excel features.

    o **Wise Owl Tutorials**: Provides comprehensive lessons on VBA and other Office applications.

This appendix connects you with valuable resources to further your learning and expand your VBA expertise, ensuring you have access to the information and support you need.

Appendix E: Sample Projects and Solutions

Practice is essential to mastering VBA, and this appendix provides a series of sample projects and solutions that demonstrate how to apply the concepts covered in this book. These projects range from beginner to advanced levels, allowing you to test and refine your skills.

1. Sample Project: Expense Tracker

- **Overview**: Automate the tracking and reporting of personal or business expenses.

- **Key Features**:

    o Automatically categorize expenses.

    o Generate monthly and yearly summaries.

    o Visualize spending patterns with charts.

- **Solution**: Includes a step-by-step guide and code snippets to build the expense tracker from scratch.

2. Sample Project: Inventory Management System

- **Overview**: Develop an inventory management tool that tracks stock levels, alerts when items are low, and generates purchase orders.

- **Key Features**:
    - Real-time stock level updates.
    - Automated reorder triggers.
    - Reporting and analysis tools.
- **Solution**: Provides the full code and explanations to implement this system in Excel.

3. Sample Project: Automated Reporting Dashboard

- **Overview**: Create a dynamic reporting dashboard that aggregates data from multiple sources and presents it in an interactive, user-friendly interface.
- **Key Features**:
    - Data consolidation from various workbooks.
    - Dynamic charts and tables.
    - User-driven filters and controls.
- **Solution**: Walkthrough of the dashboard creation process, including code for data automation and visualization.

4. Sample Project: Time Tracking and Billing System

- **Overview**: Automate the process of tracking time spent on projects and generating client invoices based on hourly rates.
- **Key Features**:
    - Time entry and tracking.
    - Automatic invoice generation.
    - Billing reports and summaries.
- **Solution**: Detailed instructions and code to set up and customize the system.

5. Sample Project: Task Management Tool

- **Overview**: Develop a task management system that assigns, tracks, and reports on tasks within a team.

- **Key Features**:

    o   Task assignment and scheduling.

    o   Progress tracking and updates.

    o   Team performance reports.

- **Solution**: Full project implementation guide with VBA code and customization tips.

These sample projects are designed to give you hands-on experience with VBA, helping you to apply what you've learned in real-world scenarios. Each project includes detailed instructions, code examples, and explanations to ensure you understand how to build and customize these solutions.

In **Part V: Appendices**, you have a wealth of resources, references, and examples at your fingertips, making this section an invaluable companion as you continue to develop your VBA skills. Whether you need a quick reference, troubleshooting help, or a practical project to test your abilities, these appendices provide the tools and guidance you need to succeed in automating and enhancing your work with Excel VBA.